Prerogatives

PREROGATIVES

Contemporary
Plays
by Women

Blizzard Publishing
Winnipeg • Buffalo

First published 1998 by Blizzard Publishing Inc.
73 Furby Street, Winnipeg, Canada R3C 2A2.

Distributed in the United States by General Distribution Services,
85 River Rock Dr., Unit 202, Buffalo, NY 14207-2170.

Cover art by Robert Pasternak.
Cover design by Otium.
Printed for Blizzard Publishing in Canada by Kromar.

5 4 3 2 1

Blizzard Publishing gratefully acknowledges the support of the
Manitoba Arts Council and the Canada Council to its publishing program.

Cataloguing in Publication Data

Main entry under title:

Prerogatives

   ISBN 0-921368-69-0

1. Canadian drama (English)—Women authors.*
2. Canadian drama (English)—20th century.*

PS8315.P747 1998   C812'.5408'09287   C98–920090–6
PR9196.6.P747 1998

CONTENTS

Preface

Earlier this year, on a slushy March day in Toronto, I met with a young woman who is writing a dissertation on Canadian feminist theatre at an Indian university. As our conversation revealed, her knowledge of Canadian theatre was extensive through volumes of published plays like this one. The publication of plays documents an aspect of Canadian theatrical culture which is clearly of interest not only to people in this country, but around the world.

Towards the end of the conversation, the Indian scholar asked, "Do you think that there is an aesthetic of woman's writing?" Ten years ago, I suspect that I would have jumped to an answer, suggesting that woman's writing eschews the linear structures of rising action and climax because those structures are modelled on male sexual arousal. Women's writing is more diffuse, metaphoric and suggestive, an excess which cannot be contained. Ten years has changed my thinking. I am no longer sure how to define women's writing, or even if it ought to be defined. Women live complex, varied lives informed not only by gender but by the negotiation of social perceptions of health, age, class, race and sexuality.

The five plays in this anthology richly illustrate this range of writing by women in contemporary Canadian theatre. Clements' *Now look what you made me do* poetically suggests the responses of women to their sexuality within the context of domestic violence. Laxdal's *Cyber:\womb*, as the playful title suggests, deals with a woman's response to infertility in the age of technology which is a force shaping all aspects of life, including fantasy. Rodin's *The Slow Eviction of Ruby Rosenholtz* deals with the lives of the marginalized suffering from severe depression—and its related illness, alcoholism—maladies which are exacerbated by poverty. Burke's *Charming and Rose: True Love* is a wry fairy tale of a woman reared by wolves who believes she is a princess destined for "true love." Miles' *I Hate You on Mondays* is a gritty depiction of three young people living in downtown Toronto.

These are five very different plays, but they have a common thread: disappointment and its commensurate emotional response, anger. Anger is a valenced response, one which emerges in different registers depending on the context. While I would no longer suggest that there is an "aesthetic" of women's writing, there may be some commonalities. As each of these plays suggests, the experience of women tends to be a local one shaped by forces over which they seem to have little control. The playwrights' approaches to depicting the lives of women vary from realistic charting (Rodin and Miles), to a lyrical fusion of reality and memory (Clements), to riffs of fantasy (Laxdal and Burke.) But underneath all of these plays, however playful and humorous, is anger. Angry women are not mad; they are enraged. Given that women still largely lack control over their lives, anger is our prerogative.

Ann Wilson,
School of Literatures and
Performance Studies in English,
University of Guelph
May 1998

Now look what
you made me do

by
Marie Clements

Now look what you made me do was workshopped and presented as a staged reading at the New Play Festival in Vancouver, directed by John Lazarus. Other staged readings include A Festival of Native Playwrights at the Illinois State University, directed by Cynthia White from the Oregon Shakespeare Festival and the Stage to Page Festival at the National Arts Centre in Ottawa, directed by Kim Selody. The play received a Fellowship Award at the Playwright's Center in Minneapolis where it was workshopped and given a staged reading directed by Randy Reinholz.

Now look what you made me do was premièred on November 10, 1995 at the Allen Theatre at the Illinois State University with the following cast:

MADONNA	Jenny Rosenburg
MAY	Francie Block
JAY	Brendan Hunt
MOTOR MAMA	Stacy Hunt
DEE	Ginger Peters
JENNIFER	Kelley Dougher
HEATHER	Alicia Hawks
The PIANO MAN	Peter Guither

Directed by Randy Reinholz
Stage Manager: Nathan King

Now look what you made me do was first produced in Canada by the Maenad Theatre at the the Big Secret Theatre in Calgary on March 8, 1996 with the following cast:

MADONNA	Nicola Elson
MAY / MOTOR MAMA	Michele Sharp
DEE	Tania Sablatash
HEATHER	Marry Ann Richards
JENNIFER / MR. HEATHER /	
JAY / MR. MOTOR MAMA	Jonathan Ryder
The PIANO MAN	Vladimir Sobolewski

Directed by Coral Larson Thew
Stage Manager: Cimmeron Meyer
Assistant Stage Manager: Anne McRae

Characters

MADONNA: A woman in her early twenties. Metis. Idealistic. New. Strong.

MAY: Madonna at twelve years old. She is dealing with the death of her father. She has a childlike quality of hope.

MOTOR MAMA: A biker chick. Tough. Large heart. Large presence. Intense. A member of the women's group.

DEE: An older prostitute. She is a friend to Madonna. She has a great sense of humour, knowing, and know-how. Sexual. Proud.

HEATHER: Somewhat religious. A housewife. A member of the women's group.

JAY: An older boyfriend of Madonna's. Abused and an abuser. This actor also plays the husbands of the members of the women's group.

JENNIFER: Housewife. Perfectionist. Self-deprecating. A member of the women's group.

PIANO MAN: An older piano man and Madonna's father.

A Note on Casting

It is recommended the play be cast with character doubling according to the following groupings:

MADONNA (a single character)
MAY and MOTOR MAMA
DEE and HEATHER
JENNIFER and JAY (as well as the husbands of the women's group)
The PIANO MAN (a single character)

If full casting is possible, additional scenes have been added to support an eight member cast. These scenes are set off in the text by square brackets [ ].

11

Set and Production Notes

The set is domestic white, made of bathrooms, kitchens, bedrooms—a porcelain look. There are many faucets with clear pipes of exposed liquid. The liquid passes through and intensifies with the colour and the rhythm of the play. The walls are white but can reveal shadows that are below or behind the surface. An old record player is in Dee's bedroom.

There should be a feeling of isolation, of being watched, of transparency. There is intensified detail of memory or fear, in the touch and sound of the environment.

Characters interact with each other but establish their own individual safe space on stage. At times they speak in unison, like a chorus.

Piano and water sounds can be done live, Billy Holiday on record.

(MADONNA is found onstage in the bathroom. DEE is in the bedroom, flooded in red light. JAY is centrestage, looking at MADONNA. MAY is close to the PIANO MAN, intent on him.)

MAY: I believed in everything up until I was thirteen.

MADONNA: I believed in almost everything after thirteen.

MAY: I believed death was very possible anywhere, anytime.

MADONNA: And it wasn't death that scared me so much, it was your death or her death or my neighbour's death or my cat. I didn't know we could die in pieces daily.

MAY: I didn't know.

(DEE sits down on the bed and unpacks her bag, placing sex toys around the bed. She cleans them herself.)

DEE: Some people die every day in pieces.

MADONNA: I'm sure Dee did. I wonder if she ever stopped dying. I wonder if everytime she slept with another john she'd die just a little more. Piece by piece. Flesh ripping raw in their grabby hands leaving her gaping just a little more. Blood seeping bright and crimson on the sheets spunked out with sperm fishing to death. Just trying to piece it all together man.

(The PIANO MAN plays softly.)

My dad used to sing … harmonize—

MAY: —He bought me a piano one day out of the grey. It was raining, coming down so hard that there was no way he could have protected it while him and some other guy tried to bring it up the old stairs into the house. The plastic tied to it was an orange, orange and it was flapping in the wind. The rain made everything shiny. It made the piano look like a black stallion coming up the stairs … charging into the house. I thought for a minute I'd finally gotten my pony. But it was a piano, all right …

(The PIANO MAN plays scales.)

… Every day, an hour a day.

13

MADONNA and MAY: *(Together, as a chorus.) Up and down the scales.*
Like a rider on the hills galloping—
  (The PIANO MAN's scales go into "If You Were the Only Girl in the
  World." The PIANO MAN sings, and then JAY takes over.)

PIANO MAN: *(Singing.)* If you were the only girl in the world—

MADONNA and MAY: *(Singing, together.)* And you were the only boy—

PIANO MAN (as DAD) and JAY: *(Singing, together.)* Nothing else would
matter in the world today ...
  (JAY moves closer to MADONNA as she sings. They sing to each
  other. MAY moves closer to the PIANO MAN.)

MADONNA: *(Singing.)* We could go on living in the same old way—

JAY: *(Singing.)* A garden of Eden just made for two—

MADONNA: It was his favorite song.

JAY: I saw her standing there. She never looked twice.
Just once. She never looked away. A straight
ahead look. No apologies. I liked that.

She believed she felt the earth under her feet.
She believed the rain baptized her.
She believed a promise was a promise.
She believed love was love. Forever.
She believed I was something good.
I wanted to believe in something, anything, for a change.
  (The PIANO MAN plays the intro to "The Lone Ranger." JAY goes
  to MADONNA.)
Hi.

MADONNA: Hi. Ho.

JAY: Pardon me.

MADONNA: Hi. Ho. Silver.

JAY: I don't get it.

MADONNA: I don't think the Lone Ranger did either.

JAY: What do you mean?

MADONNA: Look at the guy. He wore a mask all the time. He was
probably butt-ugly. And he was probably damaged.

JAY: Damaged?

MADONNA: I think the guy jumped on too many horses from high places.
Every time you watch that show he's jumping off the cliff onto poor
Silver's back. It can't be good for the ... you know.

JAY: What would you know about what's good or bad for the "you know."

MADONNA: Nothing. Just thinking.

JAY: I take it you don't like the Lone Ranger.

MADONNA: It's nothing historical. Really. The guy was just stupid.

JAY: You probably would have wanted to be Tonto.

MADONNA: Oh, there's a real treat. "Yes, Key-Mo-Saw-Be. No, Key-Mo-Saw-Be. Over there, Key-Mo-Saw-Be." End of show.

JAY: Well, you have no shoes on.

MADONNA: Oh, so that all of a sudden makes me some Tonto ... Okay, ugly.

JAY: How come you're not wearing shoes?

MADONNA: I don't like them.

JAY: I love shoes. Fine leather. Shined to perfection. It shows a man. I was in the navy for awhile. They really like shoes. Shined. Shirts pressed stiff and white, creases so sharp you could cut something on them as you walked by. I iron. It shows a man. I shine my shoes. It shows a man.

MADONNA: Hey, relax, eh?

JAY: Shoes are important, though, you can tell a man by his shoes ... ask your mother ... A man's shoes shows his character. She knows.

MADONNA: I don't like my feet all bound in. Toes all mushed together and pointy. I can't feel anything. I can't feel the ground under my feet—

JAY: How Indian did you say you were?

MADONNA: I didn't. But I'm half. Sometimes I think it's all in my feet.

(She starts to run. He trys to catch her.)

MADONNA: Look how fast I can run. Come on ... Faster than a speeding bullet. Faster than Nikes. Faster than the Lone Ranger ... Faster than—

(He catches her. They fall to the ground. He goes to kiss her. She stops him. He helps her up.)

JAY: She made me wait to touch her. I waited till I thought I was going to explode. When she was ready. She simply handed me a condom. I exploded.

(He takes her in his arms, they kiss.)

DEE: I always knew about sex. It was a sure thing. Steps slow. Daddy. Daddy. Bedspread white. Bedspread white with knobs that stood out in a pattern. I used to trace my fingers over the bedspread, eyes squinting shut, and pretend I was a blind kid figuring out a secret message, as my father traced his fingers over me, figuring out what? I don't think he had a secret message in his fingertips, do you? I think he had a secret in his penis. I figured that out too. I figured that out real good, made it into a business. It's a sure thing, you can bank on it.

(She hands MADONNA a condom.)

MADONNA: What do I do with this?

(DEE points to JAY's penis.)

Uooo. You mean I have to put it over *it*. I'm gonna die.

DEE: Are you on the pill?

MADONNA: Get serious, I went to a Catholic school.

DEE: Well then, you have to put it on.

MADONNA: What if I want to ... you know—

DEE: What?

MADONNA: You know ... blow jobs—

DEE: Then don't put the condom on. Or put the condom on with your mouth ... and do it with a condom on.

MADONNA: You mean I have to put the condom on with my mouth on ... *it*.

DEE: Well, sunshine, you're gonna have to touch it no matter what you do.

MADONNA: Great. I'm gonna feel like an idiot.

DEE: Relax. What you do is touch it first.

MADONNA: Shit.

DEE: Get to know it. Make it your friend.

MADONNA: Shit.

DEE: It's not that bad. Why don't you just try intercourse first before you become a blow job expert?

MADONNA: I just wanna know how to do it so I won't feel stupider than I already am.

DEE: Okay, here ...

(DEE reaches into her bag and pulls out a banana.)

MADONNA: What feed him a banana? What, men are really monkeys? My worries are over.

DEE: I'm gonna show you how to give a blow job. You can practice.

MADONNA: With a banana.

DEE: With a banana.

MADONNA: Why do you have bananas in your kit? Never mind, I don't want to know.

DEE: Peel the banana.

(DEE peels the skin off.)

MADONNA: Peel the penis.

DEE: *(Giving her a look.)* Hold this for a minute.

MADONNA: Great.

(DEE goes into her bag, pulls out a condom, and unwraps it. MA-DONNA takes a bite of the banana.)

DEE: Rule number one: never bite the banana.

MADONNA: Yeah, I lost a good two inches. Never bite the banana. How about just a hungry nibble.

DEE: Not even a nibble.

MADONNA: I wonder if anybody's ever bitten it off. "Ah, sorry hon, I don't know what got into me."

DEE: Are you with me here?

(DEE slips the condom into her mouth and puts it on the banana.)

MADONNA: Shit, you're a pretty good condom putter-oner.

DEE: Your turn.

MADONNA: I'm not using the same banana. They got a name for something like that. A threesome. A menage eh trois. Gross.

DEE: Here's your own banana, idiot.

MADONNA: This guy really got ripped off. Poor little thing. I can't eat him, he looks so sad.

DEE: Peel him.

MADONNA: Peel him. Right. Oh, God, do I have to.

DEE: It's only a fucking banana.

MADONNA: It's only a *fucking* banana.

(She starts making moaning noises and movements with the banana.)

The amazing fucking banana. Brought to you by the Chickeeta chick—

DEE: Now put the condom in your mouth.

MADONNA: I am not putting a condom in my mouth. Period.

DEE: Okay, skip the condom. Try licking the penis.

MADONNA: The banana.

DEE: Okay, the banana. You can lick its sides.

(MADONNA holds it out and looks at it.)

MADONNA: You can lick its sides—

DEE: You can put your mouth over it.

MADONNA: You can put your mouth over it—

DEE: You can suuuck—

MADONNA: You can make it walk—

>*(She takes the banana and struts it walking.)*

Do … do … do … do … How ya doin' Fred? Me, I'm just fine … Just other day I was saying to Bertha … geez, we should give Harriet and Jim a call … do do do … walking down the street … "*Hey,* hey we're the monkeys …"

>*(It breaks and falls to the floor.)*

Oh shit, I killed it.

DEE: Try CPR. You know, mouth-to-mouth resuscitation.

MADONNA: Very funny.

>*(They look down at the banana sadly.)*

DEE: Poor thing didn't have a chance.

MADONNA: Bad banana.

>*(She squishes it with her foot.)*

End of my blow job lesson.

>*(DEE goes back to the bed and picks out a vibrator and begins to masturbate in the shadows. We look at mirrors above her bed. There is an image of a man on top of her. JAY walks in behind MADONNA. MADONNA hears his footstep and stops him in mid-step.)*

Nice shoes, sailor.

>*(MADONNA gets up and goes towards him. She touches his shoes with her feet and then places her feet on his shoes. He begins to move with her on him.)*

JAY: I'm not a sailor. The army. The army.

MADONNA: The army, the navy … whatever. The Army and Navy. Cheap shoes. You can get cheap shoes at the Army and Navy.

JAY: Really?

MADONNA: Would I lie to you.

JAY: You better not.

MADONNA: These give a good ride, though. Like a leather saddle for my feet.

JAY: Great. My old army shoes give good ride.

MADONNA: I know what would give a better ride.

JAY: You're dangerous.

MADONNA: Why?

JAY: Because I love you.

MADONNA: How much?

JAY: It's huge.

MADONNA: Ouch.

JAY: You're weird.

MADONNA: Everybody else is weird and I'm normal.

JAY: Is that what you think?

MADONNA: That's my theory and I'm sticking to it.

JAY: Take your clothes off.

MADONNA: Take your shoes off—

JAY: A girl after my own feet.

MADONNA: Take them off ... please.

JAY: What I don't do for you ... You just don't wear shoes all the time because you have beautiful feet ... my feet on the other hand look li—sh—

MADONNA: They are gorgeous. You should let them breathe more often, that's all. See, they are breathing.

JAY: It does feel kinda good.

MADONNA: See. Okay now stand up straight ... See, they like it. Wiggle them around—

JAY: Yooowooo. I feel good!

MADONNA: Okay now calm them down.

JAY: Down feet ... down feet.

(She climbs back on them.)

So what do you call this?

MADONNA: The naked foot dance.

JAY: I shouldn't have asked.

MADONNA: How much do you love me again?

JAY: Hugely.

MADONNA: You promise.

JAY: I promise.

MADONNA: I love you.

(Lights fade on them as he raises her leg slowly up his body and wraps it around his waist, and then does the same with the other. He lifts her and kisses her as he spins slowly. He eases her slowly down his body, and exits. She is left standing a bit dizzy from the movement.)

The first time he hits you is like the first time you made love. Only different.

The first time I made love was to the music of Joan Armitrading and the mechanics of my record player rising the record up and up, slowly ... slowly ... mmmm ... precisely ... it flopping into place ... the arm rising itself slowly over and down, down, down, till it clamped down abruptly and the music started ... and spun and spun.

The same side of the record played over and over. I wondered if he knew another song.

I wondered if this was the way it always was or was somebody fucking up major here. After waiting so long to feel just this, I wondered why I had waited. I wondered if Dee felt like this everytime she took a guy to bed. That it was nothing really. She—just lying there as he pumped it up adding a moan for good measure. I wondered a lot that night. All I knew was there was one hundred and sixteen ceiling tiles. That was before I knew what making love was.

Dee told me about fucking.

Jay taught me about love.

(The mirrored image fades. DEE gets up and puts a record on the old record player. Billy Holiday's "Lover Man" plays softly, barely audible.)

DEE: Billy Holiday is somebody you play when you know you're not going to make it outside today. When you know there is no outside even if you were out.

(DEE listens to Billy. MADONNA draws closer to JAY.

MAY interrupts the PIANO MAN and begins to play the harmony of "If You Were the Only Girl in the World.")

JAY: I had this dog once when I was a kid. My mother gave it to me after months of whining. Patch. Patch was a mutt. A white dog with a patch of black over his eye. I loved that dog ... it loved me. It slept with me. It followed me to school and would wait out in the field till recess. Till lunch. Till after school. I'd run out to see him. He was a smart dog. He could talk. Slap five with his paws even play dead dog. I'd point my hand like a gun. Boom!

Dead dog!

He'd roll to the ground. Still.

Head down!

He'd lie there dead. Then he'd look up real slow. For approval ... Come here. He'd jump to me. I'd kneel down. He'd lick my face. Damn that was a loyal dog. Wouldn't do anything for anybody else. A dog is a man's best friend. Aren't you, Patch?

(The PIANO MAN takes over and begins to play "Lover Man" softly. MAY begins to sing "Lover Man" softly with it and under.)

When my parents would argue. I'd close the door real silent. And sit against it. Patch would curl up into my lap. He'd lick my face as my father would flatten his hand and slap my mother's face around the kitchen. I'd squeeze that dog tight. I'd squeeze that dog tight. It would whimper. I'd squeeze that dog tight. It felt warm against my chest. It loved me. One time I couldn't take it any more. I was a man. I was seven years old and was gonna take on my father. I got up from behind the door. Fists clenched. Patch behind me. My father looked up mid-slap.

What you doin' boy?

MADONNA: Fists clenched.

JAY: You wanna take me on boy? Momma's boy is gonna take me on … You raised yourself a real tough fag boy here Flo. Fag Boy with his dog wonder.

MADONNA: Fists clenched.

JAY: You gonna hit me boy? *Come on!!*

MADONNA: Fists clenched.

JAY: He got closer … You fuckin' that dog boy? Every day I get off from work and that dog is following you and licking you like a pussy, boy? You got a thing for dog dick boy? You're son's fuckin' the dog Flo. *He's fuckin' the dog!!*

(MADONNA goes over and places her arms around him to comfort him.)

He picked me up. Strong arms lifting and hoisted me up in the air. My mother just laid there. Head down. Her eyes down. Threw me clear across the room into the kitchen cabinets. He kicked Patch straight up. And up and up. He landed. Boom! Dead dog … Head down. But he wasn't dead. Patch got up. All teeth towards my Father. I kept screaming *dead dog!! Dead dog!!* I wanted him to just lie down like the rest of us. Just lie down and play dead. He didn't. He grabbed my father's hand mid-slap. My father raised his boot, raised his boot, raised his—raised his boot, raised his boot raised his boot. Her eyes down. Her head down. My father pointed at her—my mother.

How'd you like that boy? As useless as a dead dog.

(JAY gets up abruptly.)

What are looking at?

(He stares at her.)

MADONNA: Nothing.

(He stops. He hears the music for the first time. He smiles, and goes towards her.

DEE turns up the Billy Holiday music—"Lover Man." The PIANO MAN plays louder. MAY sings louder.

JAY offers his arm to MADONNA politely. She hesitantly takes it. They begin to slowly waltz tensely. He tightens her in a strange physical waltz, hands grabbing fist-like, twisting the dance slowly, deliberately. Twisting till she is becoming more and more lifeless.

"Lover Man" is played louder. MAY gets scared and stops singing. She huddles into the PIANO MAN.)

DEE: They say when you get hit and hurt bad you see black lights ... the black lights of unconsciousness.

(Lights fade down as JAY waltzes MADONNA's limp body around the room.

Blackout.

The PIANO MAN tinkles the piano keys ... The PIANO MAN gets MAY to offset his key notes with hers as if it they are talking, as if it is their game.

The lights fade up slowly on MADONNA on the floor alone. She pulls at her clothing and hair in an attempt to get herself together. She reacts as if she has been caught doing something bad.)

MADONNA: I've always admired insane people. The ability to just check out but still have the option of reality. I believe it's a choice. I've been there at least once. It was quiet and watery. There everybody was alive in my head, they just hadn't returned yet.

MAY and MADONNA: *(Together, as a chorus.)* ... *I waited for a good year.*

MAY: I waited for him to show up. Sitting in my bedroom waiting for his car to pull up in the back of the house. For him to get out and run up the stairs all gleaming with life, looking for me ... telling me he wasn't really dead somebody had just made a big mistake ... it happens you know. It happens you know ... it happens all the time. Like *Love Story.*

(The PIANO MAN tinkles the keys like water.

MAY smiles at the PIANO MAN as if reassured he really is there. MADONNA goes into the bathroom. She lets the faucet drip. MAY follows.)

MAY: Even though I had held his hand when he died.

Even though I saw his eyes close dead.

Fluids stop.

Silence.

No rhythms.

I still waited.

I still waited even though I had been given his ashes all boxed pretty like some strange gift.

Even though I held his ashes mixed with rocks through my fingers and wondered if the pieces of rocks were my father or the ashes. How did he get so small?

How did my big muscular, logger father ever get so small. And dead.

I waited.

Nobody can get that small.

(MADONNA and MAY take out a razor blade in the bathroom. They run the bathtub faucet. It runs ... and drips red.)

MADONNA: Twice I cut my wrists, once after he died and once after Jay said he was going to kill me.

He said it with feeling.

I meant it more.

Both times I cut with razor blades sitting down by the cool floor and bathtub. Straight razor blades, the kind your father used to shave that Old Spice shaving foam from his face. Not the disposable kind by Daisy—pink and plastic and probably a bitch to get out of the handle, but hell they look good. I didn't cut deep. Just slow. Just to see if I would die immediately, if the blood would rush from my open wrists glad of an escape and fill up the bathroom like a gold fish bowl and drown me in my own self pity. It didn't. It just oozed burnt pearls. I just laughed and laughed watching it for awhile relieved to watch it flow. After all this time of just trying to live how simple it is to just die pearl after pearl ... one long proud strand. Jay didn't like it. It was like I spoiled his fun for the evening. If he didn't get to kill me nobody could.

(MAY gets up and goes to the PIANO MAN. She shows her wrists to him. He takes her hands in his comforting them. MADONNA tries to follow but DEE begins speaking. MADONNA stops.)

DEE: I laugh a lot. If you have seen what I've seen you'd laugh. I laughed once for twelve days. It was a real blast.

You know when you start laughing sometimes and you can't stop. Well try it for twelve days. Just about killed me. I got arrested. I got locked up. In the same night. They thought I was laughing at them. Men hate to be laughed at, especially men in uniforms. As if it's the only thing women have to laugh at ... Men ... Well? I guess it didn't help that I was pointing. I got arrested for laughing. When they figured out they were just too fuckin' funny for me they sent me to Riverdale. And more laughs.

(MADONNA goes to DEE.)

MADONNA: Dee, I think I'm pregnant.

DEE: Are you sure?

MADONNA: No. I'm late.

DEE: For what?

MADONNA: Very funny.

DEE: Well, maybe your body's just stressed out with everything that's going on. Wait a couple more weeks and then go get checked out.

MADONNA: What if I'm going to have a baby? Do you think he would stop? Do you think he would want it? You know, love it.

DEE: Like he loves you. I hope not.

MADONNA: I think he would. I think he couldn't help but love it. Little tiny fingers and toes. Do you think that if I am pregnant it has little fingers already. That it's waving in there.

DEE: Yeah, that's exactly what I'm thinking.

(DEE turns away.)

Once a guy hits you he never stops.
Can't get enough, I guess.
Can't get enough of a good thing.

MADONNA: I thought maybe it would be the last time.
I believed it would be the last time.
Dee says there are no last times.

DEE: Women have been given the power of seeing. I'm sure of it. They can look at a perfectly fucked-up loser asshole shit and see something nobody else can.

Something gentle, or funny, or childlike.

Something, any *one* thing, that can be loved. And love it. The possibility of it existing ... glimpses ... flashes ... The believing of it existing. Whispers, confessions, patience. We pay for the power of seeing.

MADONNA: I went to a women's counseling group for women who get thrashed around a lot. Now that's depressing. It looked like we were all related.

(All characters move and distance themselves from each other and

transform into women at the women's group. Each becomes se-cluded in her own area of light. They do not look directly at each other but carry on and follow each other's story as if it is one continual story. Words in italics are spoken by all characters to-gether, as a chorus. HEATHER is the first to move in. She enters briskly in a tight perkiness, setting up chairs.)

HEATHER: Hello.

(The women's group barely nods. There is an uncomfortable si-lence.)

He—he—he ... He took the Bible off the shelf, the King James version, placed it in his hand ... a matter of serious ritual and he swore he swore on the Bible he was going to kill me. After three hours of Billy Graham I said. "Just shut up and do it." *Please ... please ... please ...*

JENNIFER: *... I have a problem of falling* ... from the tallest part of any room down. I don't wake up before I fall ... I land ... do you think that's bad luck? *... It's not so bad* ... he only does it when he's under a lot of pressure ... I'm not so smart, I make him mad ... I don't think some times ... I ran, you think you can run from me *he said* ... he said ... I ran, I have legs ... I had legs ... Horsemeat ... horsemeat ...

MADONNA: *... I look at his hands.* Strong. Beautiful. *His hands touch me.* His *hands* make love to me. His hands hold me. Protect me. Mold me. *His hands hit me.* How could his hands hit me?

JENNIFER: Hit me.

HEATHER: Hit me.

MADONNA: How?

HEATHER: Holy Mary Mother of God pray for us sinners ... *he said* I am a bad woman and God has sent him to punish me ... *punish me for my sins—*

MOTOR MAMA: Jesus! Enough!

JENNIFER: *He says—he says—*my hair looks like a piece of shit ... I can't seem to do anything right. That's my problem, I can't seem to do anything right. *I wonder why?*

MOTOR MAMA: I wonder why the sun don't shine—

HEATHER: I feel guilty Sundays ... it comes on real slow ... When I was a kid I used to snuggle up to my mother some nights and listen to the police radio before we fell asleep. *It would be dark.* The radio all tinny and breathless would screech in local crime. We would lie quiet and in fear *listening* to all the things we really didn't want to know. Things about bad men. *Listening.* Entering, robbing, *striking, raping, taking—*

MOTOR MAMA: *(As in* The Wizard of Oz.*)*—Oh my, striking, raping, taking, oh my—

HEATHER: —things about bad men ... When *we couldn't take it anymore* my mother would change the channel and Jesus's voice would belt through the vessels of another male. Voice strong ... hands reaching through the radio to grasp my sinful, sinful mind and body—

MOTOR MAMA: Holy holy.

JENNIFER: I feel guilty when he has hit me. As if everyone knows—

HEATHER: —My mother—

JENNIFER: —God—

ALL: *(Together, as a chorus.) And all the people listening in on the police radio.*

> *(They speak quietly.)*
> *I do not see.*
> *I do not look.*
> *I do not want.*
> *I do not feel.*
> *I do not hear.*
> *I do not question.*
> *I do not ask.*

> *(They speak louder, building.)*
> *I do not see.*
> *I do not look.*
> *I do not want.*
> *I do not feel.*
> *I do not hear.*
> *I do not question.*
> *I do not ask.*

MOTOR MAMA: King Asshole Version!

(All the women leave but MOTOR MAMA. She draws closer to the mirror. She mushes her face into it ... She laughs.)

Motor Mama's looking at you. Big fat fucking cow. Looking at you. I see you. I see you. So fucking tough but you can't even save ... you couldn't even save ... her ... Sleeping so quietly. So quietly like an angel. So quietly like an angel on and on. Mamma's angel on and on. Sleeping. Just didn't wake up. Nobody's fault. Nobody's fault. Who took you? Mommy let somebody take you. Bad Mama. Bad Mama.

(She spits on the mirror and leaves.

MADONNA gets up and goes to sit on the can. MAY races MA-
DONNA to it and beats her. She proceeds to take a pee.)

MADONNA: Sometimes you feel like a piece of shit.

DEE: Sometimes you could just shit.

(MADONNA moves towards Dee's bedroom. DEE is in full action
gear.)

DEE: Listen to this one. I'm out with this john.
We get a room. Normal right?
He takes his clothes off. Washes.
They always got to wash first.
So he washes. I wash.
Everybody's doing it.
Money up front. Money in the pocket.

Wham.

Bam.

*Ooooooo.Oh*ooo.

Great. Thank you very much. Come again.

Only he asks me if I want to make a little extra money.

I'm thinking ... handcuffs,
whips,
chains,
leather,
bad boy, big girl routine.

You know ... Ho Dee knows you've been a bad boy ... "Come here
right now and show me how sorry a bad boy can be."

Or maybe. Bad girl. Big man. Little big man.
Spanky. Spanky.
French maid runs around the mulberry bush.
Somebody special wants to meet you.
Spy that loved you.
Spy that sucked you.
I am an astronaut.
You are my earthling.
Lets create something green here.
Beat me.
Eat me.
Make me feel like the woman I am.
But no, he wants me to sit on his face.

MADONNA: So ... I thought you sat on a lot of men's faces.

DEE: Watch it here.

MADONNA: Well ... you know ... I didn't think that was something out there. I just thought that's what—

DEE: He didn't want me to just sit on his face ...

(A man walks across the stage. He stops.)

JOHN: I want you to *shit* on my face.

(He leaves.)

MADONNA: Just like that.

DEE: Just like that.

MADONNA: Holy shit, *really?!*

DEE: Holy *shit*, really.

MADONNA: Did you?

DEE: I tried. But do you think I could shit on him. It's hard to shit just like that you know. It's not like you can say to yourself, "I'm going to shit now without any motivation." You have to *have* to do it.

MADONNA: You couldn't even do like a little pebble shit. Just a "passing plunk on the john" shit.

DEE: Nope.

MADONNA: Not even a "I didn't know I could do it but holy shit look at that snake" shit.

DEE: Nope.

MADONNA: Not even—

DEE: Enough already.

MADONNA: Not even—

DEE: Not even.

MADONNA: What did you say to him, "Sorry sir, I can't seem to muster up a steamy one right now but—"

DEE: I just told him I couldn't shit on him.

MADONNA: Maybe he was Catholic.

(JAY enters from behind screens, a shadow figure that follows MADONNA wherever she walks, stopping when she stops. MAY follows, thinking it's her father.)

MAY and MADONNA: *(Together, as a chorus.) After he died I used to see him briefly—*

MAY: —getting into a cadillac, white finned ... I used to run to all his old hiding spots from my mother's tongue. Downstairs in the basement where fungus like tuffs of hair sprouted through the exposed ground.

And where I always wondered if it was really fungus or bodies that were buried standing up so the tops of their heads sprouted hair.

By his cot in the corner where a bottle of red awaited to console him after a hard day with the trees.

I let him go in the trees. In North Vancouver, overlooking the water. It was a warm spring day ... but he was hot in my hands making dent marks on my palms because I was holding him so tightly. I let him go ... talking, all the while dropping the daisies I had cut from the garden, on the ground where he was supposed to stay, but he swirled and left in the wind leaving ...

(MAY swirls off to the PIANO MAN. MADONNA goes into the bathroom and leans on the sink, head down, resting her face on the porcelain. She wets a towel and slides it down her face slowly. HEATHER and MOTOR MAMA will come onstage at different times. HEATHER is in the kitchen cooking, MOTOR MAMA is smoking, and JENNIFER is applying makeup in front of a mirror.

JAY walks from behind the shadows to the front and looks for MADONNA though he knows where she is. He walks over to the bedroom and the record player, and puts on Billy Holiday—"Ain't Nobody's Business." It plays softly. He dims the lamp. He walks around the living space swaying to the music.

The PIANO MAN plays "Ain't Nobody's Business."

MAY doesn't like the change in music. She gets scared and hides under the piano bench.)

JAY: *(Calling out.)* What are you doing in there?

MADONNA: *(Muttering.)* Fuck what do you think I'm doing?

JAY: What?

MADONNA: Nothing.

(MADONNA steps out from the door.)

JAY: Come here.

(She nods "no.")

Come on. Don't you want to dance?

MADONNA: No I want to barf.

(She walks towards him, towel in hand. He grabs one end from her and pulls her closer.)

JAY: Come onnn ...

MADONNA: I don't feel so good right now. Okay? We'll dance later.

JAY: I'm in the mood now.

MADONNA: Well, I'm not in the mood now.

(He grabs her.)

JAY: Get in the mood.

(He swings the towel around his neck like a scarf and grabs her in a whirlwind of a dance.)

MADONNA: Please don't Jay. Jay please don't. Jay please ... You're gonna make me sick. I'm gonna get sick on you Jay.

JAY: *(Politely.)* I make you sick. Is that what you're saying?

MADONNA: No, no ... I'm just not feeling well.

JAY: Honey Baby's not feeling well.

MADONNA: Stop it Jay. Please not now—

(JAY starts pulling her blouse off and kissing her as they dance.)

MADONNA: What are you doing?

JAY: Fuck what do you think I'm doing ... stupid bitch. Think I've gone deaf. Think I can't hear every word you say. Even the ones you don't say out loud.

(He rips her blouse off. He starts kissing her chest.)

MADONNA: Stop it. Stop it ... *stop it!!*

(He stops. They both freeze and look at each other. He takes the towel off and wraps it around her neck. He slowly twists it tighter and eases her down to the ground. MADONNA grasps for the towel. She struggles.)

JAY: I said dead dog.

(He brings the towel-leash down to the floor.)

Head down. Lie still. You're just going to hurt yourself. Lie still. Lie still. *Head down!!*

(HEATHER is in the kitchen. She drops a bowl. It smashes to the ground. The sound wakes him up. He looks right up at HEATHER.)

HEATHER: Oh, Jesus ... I'm ... Oh God ... I mean I'm sorry ... I didn't mean to disturb you. It just slipped. It just slipped from my hands.

(He gets up and wipes his hands on the towel. He throws the towel on MADONNA and kicks her in the stomach. She curls up.

JAY turns into MR. HEATHER.

He walks towards HEATHER.)

MR. HEATHER: It just slipped from your hands. It just slipped from her hands. Did you hear that Lord? Heather here says the bowl I worked my ass off to buy, and Jesus helped me buy because he gave me the strength to work my God-damned ass off … Just slipped from her hands.

(He takes her hands slowly, gently into his, raises them.)

Look at these hands Jesus. Good working hands, white as a day is long. Good working hands.

(He reaches up and touches her face. Then he squeezes her lips together gently.)

HEATHER: I'm sorry I forgot I shouldn't wear lipstick. Lipstick is for Mary Magdalenes. Lipstick is for Mary Magdalenes. Let me just wipe it off and I can finish dinner …

(MOTOR MAMA butts her cigarette out on her arm.)

MOTOR MAMA: *(Screaming.)* Ahhh—

MR. HEATHER: *(To HEATHER.)* Shhh …

(He takes the back of his hand and drags it slowly across her lips.)

We'll talk about this later.

HEATHER: *(Reciting the rosary as if repeating a mantra.)* Holy Mary Mother of God pray for us sinners now and at the hour of our death amen …

(MR. HEATHER leaves and goes to exit.)

***

[Note: For an eight actor cast, insert the following scene, otherwise continue with MOTOR MAMA's line, "Aaaah …" below.]

(MR. HEATHER catches his reflection in Jennifer's mirror. He draws closer to the back of her, becoming MR. JENNIFER. He remains intent on his image—preening himself and talking to her reflection in the mirror.)

JENNIFER: I need some money for that course I was talking to you about.

MR. JENNIFER: You need … You need … You need … What course?

JENNIFER: The course I was talking about. I thought maybe—

MR. JENNIFER: You thought? *(He laughs.)*

JENNIFER: Yeah.

(He picks up the hand brush on the table and throws it in her direction.)

MR. JENNIFER: Do something with your fuckin' hair … it looks like somebody shat in it. The Clarks will be here any minute and I got a wife that looks like she's been dippitty-doing her life away. Where's supper?

JENNIFER: I thought maybe—

MR. JENNIFER: You thought, you thought, you thought, you thought. What?

JENNIFER: I thought maybe we could go down the street to that Italian restaurant they've been wanting to try out—

MR. JENNIFER: Let me do the fucking thinking all right. Here let me make dinner all right, here let me do everything all right ... here let me fix this rat's nest ... God you look like a horse, that's it, my wife the nag.

(He grabs JENNIFER's hair and drags her over to the counter past HEATHER. He grabs a pair of scissors, and drags her back to her mirror. He goes to cut her hair. She grabs her hair. They are in a deadlock.)

JENNIFER: *(Softly.)* Don't you think that's enough.

(The doorbell rings.

MR. JENNIFER and JENNIFER freeze. HEATHER stops her mantra. They all listen.

MR. JENNIFER lets go of her hair slowly. He looks in the mirror with supreme confidence, straightening himself. He smiles into the mirror wide-mouthed and teeth flashing. MOTOR MAMA screams.)

***

MOTOR MAMA: *(Screaming.)* Aaaah ...

(The sound of MOTOR MAMA's scream draws MR. JENNIFER to her. He changes into MR. MOTOR MAMA.

HEATHER resumes reciting the rosary, as if repeating a mantra underneath the scene.)

HEATHER: Holy Mary Mother of God ...

MR. MOTOR MAMA: Don't you think that's enough. That you've pun- ished yourself enough today.

MOTOR MAMA: Make me stop.

MR. MOTOR MAMA: I can't make you stop. Only you can do that. Don't look at me like that.

MOTOR MAMA: I thought you liked Mama mad. You used to say it turned you on.

MR. MOTOR MAMA: Christ, Margaret, that's not what I'm talking about. Why the hell do you keep hurting yourself. It wasn't your fault. It was nobody's fault Margaret.

MOTOR MAMA: Don't call me Margaret or I will be upset.

MR. MOTOR MAMA: Okay, okay … Well, you look weird. That's all. That's all I'm saying.

MOTOR MAMA: Nag … nag … nag … I should come over there and give you the what for.

MR. MOTOR MAMA: What for?

(She slaps him upside the head.)

MOTOR MAMA: For shootin' your fuckin' head off about something you don't know anything about.

MR. MOTOR MAMA: Dammit Marg—Mar—Mamma, what did you do that for?

MOTOR MAMA: I don't know.

MR. MOTOR MAMA: I do know about it. I do know about it.

(He walks out.

MADONNA gets up from the floor and wipes the area where she laid with the towel; it has turned red. She starts singing softly as she takes the towel to the toilet and twists it down the drain. HEATHER gets up from kneeling down and picks up the glass pieces; she joins in. MOTOR MAMA hits herself on different parts of her body, and joins in on last part of the song.)

MADONNA: *(Singing.)* If my man ain't got no money and I say take all of mine honey, ain't nobody's business if I do.

HEATHER: *(Singing.)* I'd rather my man would hit me than for him to jump up and quit me.

(HEATHER and MADONNA look at each other in the eye and quickly look away.)

MADONNA, HEATHER [and JENNIFER]: *(Singing.)* Ain't nobody's business if I do …

MOTOR MAMA: *(Singing.)* … If I beat up on my poppa and he don't call no coppa, ain't nobody's business if I do …

(MOTOR MAMA looks at them both. They all stop in their tracks.)

ALL: *(Together, singing.)*
Nobody's business …
Ain't nobody's business …
Nobody's business if I dooo.

(Blackout. They speak together, as a chorus.)
Shut up Billy.

(The lights fade up. JAY is on the floor. MADONNA is holding him, rocking him. He is trying to sing "If You Were the Only Girl in the World" by himself. MAY gets up from under the piano bench when she hears the song. JAY gets up and leaves quietly. MAY quietly goes toward MADONNA.)

MADONNA: *(Sarcastically.)* He promised he wouldn't hit me again.
I mean he promised. Crying promise.
The kind of promise you go holy shit
he really means it promise.

MAY: Right up until the end I asked him not to die.
Not in all the words but I willed it so.

I'd sit by his bed. Day after day. And hold his hand. I figured if I held him. If I was there. There's no way he would leave. Besides he had promised.

MADONNA: He had promised he'd never leave me.

MAY: He had promised.

MADONNA and MAY: *(Together, as a chorus.) A promise is a promise ...*

(MADONNA looks for a dripping tap noise. She secures each faucet till the last one where she just watches the water dripping.)

MADONNA: If you can reach your cave, you'll be okay. Hollow out your bed and lie fetal-curled like a fern. It is dark and damp here, surfaces watering. Cave tears running down the walls in minute slowness. You watch each tear snake its river down until it reaches you adding to your liquidness. It is in the concentration of each tear which keeps you safe and covered. Sound penetrates only if you haven't concentrated.

You only have yourself to blame.

MAY: My father died, tubes opened wide to allow all the fluids in and out of his body. Gurgling like a water fountain, consistent, safe in a rhythm. A direction of up and down ... something you'd never want to put your mouth over even if your mother said it was okay. I'd sit and watch the flow from all his tubes, some clear, some red, dripping like the damn sink faucet when you're trying to sleep. Just sit and listen to that music knowing as long as everything flowed so did his life. Listen. Maybe I thought if he knew I was listening to his life he wouldn't die.

(MAY goes towards the PIANO MAN. She sits and drops the keys like water. She encourages the PIANO MAN to join in.

There are mirrors everywhere. The women's group walk towards their different areas. Their whole scene is cartoonish and huge in exaggeration. Their appearances have changed to accommodate their state of mind. HEATHER's boobs and and lips have become huge. JENNIFER's hair is permed crazy, and her body has become more male than before, complete with a big crotch. MADONNA's face and neck are red and blue blotched. MOTOR MAMA's appearance has become more menacing and her face is swollen. They set up in front of their individual mirrors with a personal choreography that reflects how they see themselves, how they feel in personal details. Words in italic are spoken by all characters, as a chorus. MADONNA just sits there after placing articles down.)

ALL: *(Together.)*
   I do not see.
   I do not look.
   I do not feel.
   I do not want.
   I do not question.
   I do not ask.
   I do not ...
   King Asshole Version.

HEATHER: Here you go honey, why don't you try this? Madonna ...?

   (Hands her a cover stick. MADONNA just looks at it.)

MADONNA: Yeah ... why don't I try this.

HEATHER: Mmmm. I love red lipstick. This is probably the only place I can wear it ... Here, you try some ... it will give you some colour.

MADONNA: I think I have enough colours, thank you.

   (HEATHER goes back to the mirror, puts red lipstick on her really big exaggerated lips and looks at her humongus boobs.)

HEATHER: He says my tits are too big. Like what the hell am I supposed to do about that. Cut them off? *Don't give him any ideas.* He says God must have made my tits big for some reason. Guess the reason? Because I was born a slut. A slut. And he was sent here so I could be made a better person. Do you know how many times a week we go to church? Five times a week. I hardly have time to work, look after the kids, cook, clean ... never mind becoming a slut.

It takes a fair amount of time to become a slut but he won't listen to reason. *He follows me everywhere.* I have to admit it is like God is everywhere. I got him back though. I cut the prongs of his zipper so when he was standing up in front of all the good people preaching his little pecker would flop out. He came home all flushed saying how they don't make anything like they used to. I just nodded my good ol' head in agreement. Amen. *Amen ...*

JENNIFER: He says I'm built like a man. Nothing right about my body. It's too big he says. He doesn't like my hair, my eyes, my nose, my ass.

Who would be with me? *He's says I'm lucky.* I'm lucky. Maybe I am. I mean he's so good-looking, everybody likes him and it doesn't happen that much. Only when I open my mouth. Do you like my mouth? I think if I wore a more peachy colour it would bring out my own colour better, what do you think? I am a Summer—

MOTOR MAMA: Honey, I think you got bigger problems than the seasons.

JENNIFER: Some days I would just like to tell him to shut up. Can you imagine? Shut up Bill. Just *like that.* Shut up! You big slob.

HEATHER: Ohh you're really letting him have it.

JENNIFER: Well I do hope every once in a while that he would be hit by a big truck. I'd go to the funeral dressed in Jackie Onassis black. *(As if at his funeral.) It is sad* ... Yes it is so sad. Such a fine man. So good looking. A great husband and father. What am I going to do? Just live day to day as best as I can. Yes, it will be hard but *that's the kinda woman I am.*

Do you think I should get a perm?

HEATHER: No more perms.

MOTOR MAMA: Fuck the perm. I say fuck the perm!

ALL: *(Together.) Fuck the perm! Fuck all perms!!*

MOTOR MAMA: I'll stick a big knife right in 'im till he can't do nothin' but scream. The bastard ... the dirty shit-picking, grimy mother. I'm not gonna wait till my man goes to sleep to do it neither. Like that woman in the paper. Waited till her ol' man was sleeping, probably snorin' or sweatin' ... and snuffed him out with a thirty-eight. Bang. Bang. You're a dead motherfucker. Too good for him if you ask me.

Or that woman who waited till her ol' man was sleeping and poured a bottle of Grand Marney on 'im and lit him up like a Christmas Pardy. Too good for 'im that's what I say. I say save your Grand Marney honey. I say why wait till they're asleep. I want him to see it coming and to see who's giving it to him ... Then I'll *drink* that Marnay.

ALL: *(Together.) Cheers! I think.*

(MADONNA takes the cover stick and whites out her face slowly. Coldly, methodically, she talks. She takes the lipstick and paints red strips across her face like Tonto war paint.)

MADONNA:
I love him.
I watch him. Every move.

The man showers in the morning. Towels himself just so. Brushes those teeth. Smoothes shaving foam on his hands. Those hands. That face. Takes the razor and logs his skin. Watches himself in the mirror. Glad his face turns just so towards the light.

I love him.

I watch him. Every move.

I wish the razor would slip.

> *(HEATHER and JENNIFER and MOTOR MAMA stare into their mirrors.)*

MOTOR MAMA: *(Whispering.)* I hate you. I hate you. I hate you ... I hate you.

> *(MOTOR MAMA continues whispering "I hate you" under the following.*
>
> *MADONNA gets up slowly, painfully, and goes to the bathroom. She lets the faucet run. She flushes the toilet in a rhythm. She listens to its sound.)*

DEE: Madonna ...

> *(MADONNA takes her hand off the toilet handle slowly. MADONNA walks to each faucet and opens them all up. She scrubs the towel over her face, trying to get the paint marks off.)*

What are you doing? Slow down ... it's okay, Everything will be okay ... Does it hurt much?

MADONNA: Only when I move or breathe.

DEE: Good sign.

MADONNA: Yah, good sign.

> *(She passes the mirror and really looks into it. Her face becomes the distorted face of MOTOR MAMA. They stare at each other. MOTOR MAMA stops whispering. They stare at each other and touch each other. MOTOR MAMA leaves. JAY is standing in seclusion, whispering, "I'm sorry," over and over under the following, and becoming louder.)*

Fuck I look like the elephant woman.

DEE: It's not that bad ... It will go down. You should get that ear checked out it's all ... anyways he could have broke your eardrum.

MADONNA: No such luck, I can still hear him.

> *(DEE covers her ears and moves back to her bed. She sits on it touching the bedspread with her hands.)*

JAY: I'm sorry ... I *am* sorry ... I'mmm sorry. I'm so sorry. So very sorry. Sorry, sorry. So. I'm ... sorry. Real sorry. Biggest realest sorry. More than sorry. I—I—I—I—Me—me—me—me—sorry ... sorry—

MADONNA: I'm—

JAY: —sorry—

MAY: That's what they said. That's all they said. I had gone to grab a pop and was coming back to his room. Just turning the knob.

JAY: I'm sorr—

MADONNA: —he's dead—

DEE: —he's dead.

MAY: Slow motion ... I looked up at the nurse all crisp and white standing there like I was the one who couldn't hear properly.

JAY: I ... am ... sorry—

MADONNA: —he's dead—

DEE: —he's dead.

MAY: All I could see really was her face ... his face mouthing those words. From where I was standing looking up ... she ... he ... looked like a pig up close. All mouth and snout ... perky teeth going.

JAY: *(Concerned.)* Madonna ...?

MADONNA: Shh ...

(The water from every faucet starts getting louder. Different colours emerge in each basin. MADONNA and MAY go to the bathtub in a daze. She talks to MAY. It is filling up with red. They touch it as one and bathe themselves in it. JAY follows her, watching.)

MADONNA: Ticking ... rain sound streams ... away ... down low ... stop ... don't ... oozing ... softly ... passing ... shhh ... shhh ... baby ... baby ...

I had a child grow inside me. It knew my caves. It cried there. I had wanted to see the best of ourselves. I had wanted to ... listen ... smashed ... knock ... stop ... stop ... The child left liquid ... Echoes of small child feets on my walls. The child left just like liquid.

(MADONNA leaves the bathtub and embraces the toilet. The round smoothness of the toilet appears attached to her like a pregnant stomach.)

It's down with the crocodiles now ... Sh ... *sh*... it's okay now isn't it? Everything's okay ... Isn't it? It's still throbbing in me, throbbing in ... me ... breathing ... dripping ... dripping its breath ... its blood. Numb. Numb. Nummmb.

JAY: Madonna ...? I'm sorry.

MADONNA: You've died inside me.

JAY: What?

MADONNA: You've died inside me.

   (Pause.)

JAY: What do you mean, "You've died inside me ..." What do you mean? What died? *What died?!*

MADONNA: You made it die inside me ... If only I could have held its hand ... its tiny ... tiny hand. Fists clenched. Fists clenched. Fingers already clenched to fight. I would have liked to kiss his fingers.

JAY: What baby?

MADONNA: I can't talk about it right now. It's not a good time to talk about it right now.

DEE: *(To JAY.)* Fuck off.

MAY: *(To JAY.)* Fuck off.

   (He touches her softly.)

MADONNA: Please don't.

JAY: Don't move away from my touch. Please don't.

MADONNA: Not again.

JAY: You're a liar. You're a liar. What baby? There was no baby, you didn't say anything about a baby. You're lying to me.

   You are lying to me!!

   Take your clothes off and let me see. I want to see for myself.

MADONNA: *(Smiles oddly.)* You can't see everything.

JAY: Take your clothes off.

   (DEE stands in seclusion in her bedroom. She starts taking off articles of her clothes as if she is with a john or her father. She starts breathing like she is having sex.)

JAY: *I said take your clothes off!!*

MADONNA: No.

MAY: I said *no.*

JAY: Take your fuckin' clothes off or so fuckin' help me—

DEE: Help him?

JAY: So fuckin' help me I'll ... fucking kill you. Do you understand?

MADONNA, MAY and DEE: *(Together, as a chorus.)* I hear you.

   [The women's group mouths "I hear you," some more audibly than others. They all echo the words under. They all close their eyes as if knowing what is to come. They all listen. In their own worlds they decide to stay with him or leave him on stage alone.]

(*MAY and MADONNA start removing their wet clothes, piece by piece. The lights on the three women become spotted and appear as bruises mixed with blood on their bodies. Their movements are trancelike.*

The sound of water pumping increases in volume and overflows. The sound of sex-breathing coming from DEE is increasing. The sound of Billy Holiday is distorted.)

MADONNA:
smashed
slowly
softly
pounding

MAY:
don't
don't
squashed
softly

DEE:
fingers pushing through my skin
someplace normal

MAY:
hear a voice?
mushy ... mushy
there's no more

MADONNA:
maybe I'm dead
I can't stop
passing
blood
pressure in my head

DEE:
don't touch me
there is no more someplace normal
fingers pushing through my skin

DEE, MAY, and MADONNA: (*Together. as a chorus.*) I loved you ...

[HEATHER and JENNIFER: (*Together.*) I loved you.]

[MOTOR MAMA: I love you.]

(*The sound of water stops. The sound of sex-breathing stops. The sound of Billy stops. The sound of a distorted electronic buzz begins.*)

MAY: I loved you—

MADONNA: —Please don't die—Don't die—

MAY: —Please. I'll do anything. Just don't die—

MADONNA: —I was going to look after you when you got old—

MAY: —Remember—

MADONNA: —Please don't die and leave me here alone—

MAY: Please.

MADONNA: I loved you—

DEE: There were pieces everywhere.
Sometimes you can only live if a part of you dies.

*(The light bruises fade. MAY, DEE and MADONNA turn in unison
and leave. The lights on JAY form bruises on his body. He discovers
them and is horrified. He touches them. He sits himself in the doorway rocking himself.*

*The PIANO MAN plays a distorted version of "If You Were the Only
Girl in the World," the piano clunking.)*

JAY: I love you ... I love you ... I loved you ... You loved. I, I, me, me,
me, I love you I love you ... You love ...

*[One by one JAY directs his attention to the women's group. MO-
TOR MAMA leaves in disgust. JENNIFER carefully packs her stuff
and leaves. HEATHER kneels to begin praying.]*

... I love you I love you ... You love ...

(The end.)

Cyber:\womb

by
Vivienne Laxdal

Cyber:\womb was originally developed with commissions from the Great Canadian Theatre Company and the National Arts Centre. Further assistance was granted by the Ministére de la culture du Quebec.

Cyber:\womb was first produced by the National Arts Centre's Atelier Workshop Programme in November, 1994, with the following cast:

ONEIDA	Missy Christensen
ROBERT	Chip Chuipka
SISTER	Nadine Desrochers
MAUREEN / PRIME MINISTER	Mary Ellis
CLERK / CINDY / DIANE	Victoria Hammond
DR. KRUMM / BODY GUARD / DR. EPSON / RECEPTIONIST	Paul Rainville
MICHAEL	Ryan Laxdal
CHRISSY	Brittany Wilson

Directed by Gil Osborne
Set and Slide Design by Geoff Levine
Lighting Design by John Munro
Original Music and Sound Design by Marc Desormeaux
Costume Design by Simone MacAndrew
Assistant Director: Anne Troake
Stage Manager: Rebecca Miller
Production Assistant: Lynn Cox
Cyber:\womb created by c.j. fleury
Slide Consultant: David Lepage

Cyber:\womb was the 1995 winner of the Dave Smith Ottawa Valley book Festival Playwriting Award.

Characters

Main Characters

ONEIDA: Oneida Kilborn (pronounced "O-nye´-da") is thirty-four years old and works in an office. She is not overly concerned about her appearance—she likes to be comfortable. Leggings and loose tops are her clothes of choice. She and Robert have been married for seven years, and have been actively trying to conceive a baby for the past four years. They began in vitro fertilization cycles almost a year ago. So far, two attempts have failed. The year has been extremely draining to her both emotionally and physically.

ROBERT: Robert Kilborn, forty years old, works in a managerial position for a small software company. He appears to be making every attempt to cope responsibly with their situation—to supply Oneida with the proper support and encouragement. He and Oneida have struggled through the economic reality of the times, and still reside in the garden-home which was only to be temporary after they married.

SISTER: She appears to be about the same age as Oneida. As a child, Oneida created an imaginary sister for companionship, but upon learning that her mother aborted a pregnancy prior to Oneida's conception, Sister became for her the spiritual manifestation of that potential life. Sister is an obvious physical contrast to Oneida both in the way she carries herself and dresses. She exudes sexuality and confidence. Their physical and mental comfort when together is overt and familiar. There is no such thing as "personal space" between them.

Nobody is aware of Oneida's relationship with her Sister. When they appear together on the stage their interaction is invisible to the other players.

Recurring Characters

MAUREEN: Oneida's mother, in her late fifties. In her youth, she was an Olympic bronze-medallist skier. Although she loves Oneida, she has never been particularly comfortable or happy in the role of mother.

DR. KRUMM: An obstetrician and infertility specialist. His services are in high demand.

Secondary Characters
CLERK: She works in a children's clothing store and is visibly pregnant.
PRIME MINISTER: A pregnant woman in her late forties, due any minute.
DR. EPSON: A psychiatrist, pregnant.
CINDY: Oneida's co-worker, a new mother.
DIANE: A female executive, pregnant.
RECEPTIONIST: She works in Dr. Krumm's office, pregnant.
MARTY MINKO: A teenage football jock.
BODYGUARD: Bodyguard to the Prime Minister.
Two NURSES: Both pregnant.

Voiceovers
INTERCOM (in the hospital)
RADIO NEWS READER (CBC)
MICHAEL, a seven-year-old child.
CHRISSY, a seven-year-old child.

The following suggestion for doubling of roles will work for a cast of four women and two men:

ONEIDA (a sole character)
SISTER (a sole character)
ROBERT and MARTY MINKO
DR. KRUMM, BODYGUARD, DR. EPSON, and RECEPTIONIST
MAUREEN, PRIME MINISTER, and a NURSE
CLERK, CINDY, DIANE, and a NURSE

A Note on Staging

The text calls for visual effects of sperm and egg cell activity and embryo development. These may be used as a device to underscore and bridge the ends and beginnings of scenes.

Design and performance should support Oneida's ascension into her cyber-world madness, particularly in Act Two. Sister's costume gradually changes to reflect Oneida's concepts of "Cyberpunk." Dr. Epson and the Receptionist should appear as full-blown "cyber-characters"—the purpose of having the actor who plays Krumm play these roles is that it reflects Oneida's growing paranoid delusion.

Act One

Scene One

(Oneida's bedroom, four a.m.

ONEIDA is slowly performing upper-body callisthenics with riveting intensity. ROBERT is in bed. He wakes and stretches. ONEIDA gradually works herself into a light jog, emphasizing her words with punchy arm movements.)

ROBERT: What are you thinking about?

ONEIDA: Eggs.

ROBERT: I take it you don't mean the breakfast kind.

ONEIDA: You know what one of those husbands said at our last I.C. group session?

ROBERT: This would be that lawyer, right?

ONEIDA: Why would that woman want to have his child, anyway?

ROBERT: What did he say?

ONEIDA: He said that we should be "grateful—g*rateful*—that there are selfless women out there, willing to donate their eggs."

ROBERT: Well, it's not an easy process for a woman—

ONEIDA: With that condescending tone.

ROBERT: Not like going into the bathroom with a magazine and a cup.

ONEIDA: I wanted to reach across the circle and slap him.

ROBERT: That Infertile Couples Group was a crock, anyway.

ONEIDA: Grateful. Yes, I am so grateful. Grateful that there is some anonymous woman out there with eggs to share ... eggs to spare! What is she anyway, some kind of humanoid chicken on a factory farm?

(Pause.)

ROBERT: Why can't you read when you wake up in the middle of the night, like everybody else?

(She stops jogging.)

47

ONEIDA: I'm sorry.

ROBERT: 'S all right. I had to get up in two hours, anyway ... C'mere.

(ROBERT pulls her to him. He holds her.)

ONEIDA: Three strikes and we're out of there, Robert. This is the third pitch.

ROBERT: I knew I shouldn't have turned you on to baseball.

ONEIDA: I was no virgin to the sport.

ROBERT: Lucky for me—I didn't have to explain the rules.

(ROBERT caresses her sexually. She stops him.)

ONEIDA: What are you doing?

ROBERT: I am driven wild by the aroma of your sweaty nightgown.

ONEIDA: I'll go take a shower.

ROBERT: The morning is but young! You can have a shower at hey, five o'clock.

ONEIDA: Sex doesn't make sense.

ROBERT: Sex makes sense. Lots of sense.

ONEIDA: Sex is supposed to make babies, Robert.

ROBERT: Sex doesn't just have to make babies.

ONEIDA: It does after you've been trying for three years ... maybe two, maybe one! I think we've had too much sex. Seven years of sex!

ROBERT: There was a time when you would call me at work. "Robert ... I'm up a degree." I'd have to make up an excuse to leave the office. "It's an emergency! I have to go home and service the wife." That was fun. Intimidating. But fun. Why don't we just relax a bit, hmm?

(ONEIDA squirms away from him.)

ONEIDA: I relax best in the shower.

Scene Two

(The bathroom.

In the mirror, ONEIDA is studying herself. SISTER appears on the other side.)

SISTER: So, how many are they sticking in you this time?

ONEIDA: Three.

SISTER: That doctor ... what's his name?

ONEIDA: Krumm. Dr. Krumm. K–R–U–double-M.

(SISTER comes around the mirror to beside ONEIDA.)

SISTER: In Vitro King, at your service.

(DR. KRUMM appears in the mirror.)

DR. KRUMM: We have established the nature of the problem, Mrs. Kilborn.

ONEIDA: *(To DR. KRUMM.)* I recently read of a fifty percent decrease in the modern-day-man's sperm-count.

SISTER: Two to three million per ejaculation does not a deficit make.

DR. KRUMM: Ovarian scarring has disabled your productivity.

ONEIDA: He means it's me.

DR. KRUMM: I prefer to counsel my patients to accept their infertility.

ONEIDA: I can't make a baby.

DR. KRUMM: However, this IVF clinic has the highest live-birth success rate in all of the province.

ONEIDA: I'm the one.

DR. KRUMM: If you would carefully read this contract, and you and your husband sign—

SISTER: Make sure you read the small print.

DR. KRUMM: Now, to begin we will need to know the first day of your menstrual cycle for the next three thousand months ...

(He disappears.)

SISTER: *You* know why this is happening.

(MARTY appears in football gear.)

MARTY: Heyyy ... Oneida, Baby! *Porky's* is on at the drive-in!

SISTER: Marty Minko.

ONEIDA: I believed him when he said he could stop himself.

MARTY: Whoops.

SISTER: Everyone knew when you threw up at morning assembly.

MARTY: Hey, it could've been anyone! Ask Johnny ... he took her out the week before!

ONEIDA: I didn't have enough in my savings, the woman at the clinic said it would cost—

MARTY: Two hundred bucks? Forget it! I gotta fix my car!

(He disappears.)

ONEIDA: At Girl Guides, they taught you how to be resourceful.

(SISTER looks to a stool. ONEIDA climbs on to it and jumps and lands hard. MAUREEN appears. ONEIDA continues to jump through the following.)

MAUREEN: Oneida, I know what you're trying to do ... Believe me, I know!

SISTER: Mother had a trick or two of her own.

MAUREEN: We can fix it. I know someone ... he helped me once ... I'll make an appointment.

SISTER: She would, too.

MAUREEN: Who was it? Who? Has he accepted any responsibility for this? I am going to kill that little bastard!

SISTER: She could, too.

MAUREEN: Oh, for Christ's sake, Oneida, didn't they teach you anything in health class?

(ONEIDA suddenly clutches herself and cries out in pain.)

MAUREEN: So stupid! ... why didn't you just ... it can be so simple!

(MAUREEN disappears.)

SISTER: Where there's a will ...

ONEIDA: I was pregnant once. It could happen again. Please, let it happen again. And this time, I'll protect it.

I promise. I will protect it!

(Visual: human egg surrounded by sperm.)

Scene Three

(The day-surgery corridor in a hospital.

ONEIDA is laying on a gurney with her knees bent. ROBERT is sitting on the edge of the bed. He is playing a Gameboy. Enter DR. KRUMM with his clipboard.)

DR. KRUMM: My apologies for having you recover out here in the corridor, Oneida—everything else is occupied. Now, I trust you are familiar with the routine. Simply lie still, knees up, and relax for a while.

INTERCOM: Dr. Krumm to obstetrics, please ... Dr. Krumm to obstetrics.

DR. KRUMM: I'll come and check on you in a bit.

(ROBERT continues to play as ONEIDA speaks.)

ONEIDA: Everything is numb.

ROBERT: Hm?

ONEIDA: I'm just one, big, old, numb uterus. *(Coaxing.)* Come on, come on, you can do it. Look at that comfy lining, wouldn't you like to just snuggle in there and put your feet up. All warm and ... nourishy.

Robert. Robert.

ROBERT: *(Losing his game.)* Shit!

ONEIDA: Look, I know we're old hands at this, but could you at least feign more interest in our potential conception than in attaining a higher level in Tetris?

ROBERT: Sorry. *(He playfully stares at her, expectantly.)* How's this?

ONEIDA: Oh, forget it. Can I play?

ROBERT: I can't save it. Magazine?

> *(ROBERT hands her a* Time *magazine—January, 1994—and continues to play.)*

ONEIDA: *(Reading.)* "Genetics. The Future is Now." You know, I'm sick of being told I'm a card in the hands of fascist science. I'm not into eugenics. I just want a baby.

> *(SISTER appears.)*

SISTER: It is quite amazing what they can do now, isn't it?

ONEIDA: I suppose.

SISTER: Eradication of genetic disease, elimination of undesirable traits, and promotion of the trendy, all possible with a little recombinant nip and tuck of the DNA.

ONEIDA: That's genetic therapy, you moron. I'm just trying to get pregnant.

SISTER: One intervention leads to another. The pharmaceutical consortium is having a party with all you infertiles. Mark my words. Pretty soon, they're going to have laws about breeding.

ONEIDA: What am I, a cocker spaniel?

SISTER: Woof, woof.

ROBERT: Uh, I have to call the office ... you want something from the caf'?

ONEIDA: No.

ROBERT: You'll be all right alone?

ONEIDA: Don't be long, okay?

> *(Exit ROBERT.)*

SISTER: You do have to admire him. Never once has he made a noise about it.

ONEIDA: About what?

SISTER: All these years you and your little man have struggled to save enough for a down payment on a house, and pouf! All gone now on your little whimsies.

ONEIDA: It's a question of priorities. There will always be houses to buy.

SISTER: But no "woom to gwow in"? *(Pause.)* Why would anyone wish to bring a child into this sick and troubled world, anyway?

ONEIDA: With a proper upbringing this child—or these children—may do something great.

SISTER: Oh, so it's child*ren*, now?

ONEIDA: There's a good chance it'll be twins.

SISTER: Twins! At this time of economic woe, political uncertainty, unemployment, AIDS, wars—

ONEIDA: They may help our world! They might be great environmentalists, or writers or—

SISTER: They might also keep ol' Bobby in place.

ONEIDA: That's really tacky, you know that?

SISTER: Seven years of marriage, right? What's going to keep him from scratching if he's got nothing to tickle his fancy at home?

ONEIDA: You know, even when we were little you undermined everything I did.

SISTER: Not true!

ONEIDA: Like when I entered the public speaking contest in grade seven, and I got a standing ovation. You said it was because they felt sorry for me because Dad had been caught in a scandal and had left us.

SISTER: Well, they did! It was all over the papers!

ONEIDA: They liked my speech!

SISTER: Okay, okay. Oneida, look. One question. What are you going to do if it doesn't work this time?

(Re-enter DR. KRUMM.)

DR. KRUMM: Well, how are we doing?

INTERCOM: Dr. Krumm to Obstetrics please ... Dr. Krumm.

(He helps ONEIDA up.)

DR. KRUMM: Okay, now. Take it easy for a few days, no heavy lifting or running, or jumping about. Call me if you experience any pain or bleeding.

ONEIDA: I have a headache!

DR. KRUMM: Abdominal or uteral discomfort only, Mrs. Kilborn. Take a Tylenol. I'll see you in two weeks.

Scene Four

(A children's clothing store in a mall. Christmas music plays under. ONEIDA is browsing.)

CLERK: Lovely day.

ONEIDA: It's freezing rain.

CLERK: Oh! Is it? Well, that's the great thing about shopping in malls. You're never at the mercy of the weather.

ONEIDA: Right.

CLERK: What is the weather like out there, anyway? *(Beat.)* Oh ... right. Shoot. I'm not very good at this—

ONEIDA: Pardon me?

CLERK: It's just ... you see, we have a new manager, and she wants us to use the "soft sell" approach. We're supposed to make the customer feel at ease ... never say, "May I help you ..." but slowly and subtly draw their attention to our winter collection.

ONEIDA: Oh. Well, honestly I wasn't thinking of buying anything ... I was ... just getting a feel for it.

CLERK: Oh. *(Pause.)* "Getting a feel for it ..." Are you expecting, then?

ONEIDA: Well ... maybe.

CLERK: You mean you're not sure, yet?

ONEIDA: I'm not certain, no.

CLERK: Oh! You have no idea how *relieved* I am to hear you say that! Almost every mother I know says she knew the second it happened ... she felt it.. she felt different, she *knew* she was carrying.

Not only that, she also knew the sex. Right away. She had his name, layette and wallpaper all picked out and put up before he even reached his second trimester because she knew! Gag me.

(ONEIDA is admiring a bunting bag.)

ONEIDA: These are adorable.

CLERK: Oh, yes! This is the latest in our winter infant collection by Calvin Klein ... You see, you brought it up first, so I'm allowed to talk about it now.

(ONEIDA looks at the price tag.)

ONEIDA: Ouch.

CLERK: What can I say? "Sears utilitarian" we are not.

ONEIDA: You know, I really shouldn't ... Oh, I'll go crazy. I'll take two.

CLERK: Two?

ONEIDA: Well, it might be twins.

CLERK: Oh! Do twins run in the family?

ONEIDA: No—

CLERK: Oh, but you feel it might be twins? *(Beat.)* What size?

ONEIDA: Well, by next winter they'll be about six months—

CLERK: Now, if I may make a suggestion, you should purchase size eighteen months ... what with all the growth hormones in our water table now, from the cows excretions ... have you heard about this?

ONEIDA: I'm not sure that I have.

CLERK: Let me ask you—do you plan to nurse your babies? We all know breast is best.

ONEIDA: Yes.

CLERK: Good for you. Although, undoubtedly, there will be times when you and your husband ... excuse me ... partner, mate, spousal equivalent, friend ... or are you going solo?

ONEIDA: Husband.

CLERK: Ah. Well, there will be occasions when you will wish to go out together—your anniversary for instance. You know, it's important to have time alone, away from the children, to rekindle your romance.

ONEIDA: That's what the books say.

CLERK: They also say it's very difficult to pump your own milk and freeze it properly, and on those occasions when you have a date you will probably choose to use formula. *But*, the formula, as we know, is made with water that is contaminated with these cow hormones.

It's quite incredible, actually. Infants are growing at unprecedented rates. So now, at six months, babies are wearing size eighteen months. Thus, my suggestion.

ONEIDA: Okay, size eighteen months.

CLERK: Two?

ONEIDA: Two.

CLERK: Great. I'll be right back.

(The scene fades into the sound of a radio news broadcast.)

Scene Five

(The bedroom. ONEIDA and ROBERT are in bed.)

RADIO: ... And summing up the headlines: Previously forecasted economic recovery for the nation has not measured ... will not ... uh ... isn't.

Three provincial governments announce further cutbacks to health ... care.

An unnamed twelve-year-old girl in the capital region voluntarily serving as a surrogate mother for her sixty-three-year-old aunt, gives birth to triplets weighing in at three, nine and fifteen and a half pounds.

And the Prime Minister is expecting today ... excuse me ... expected today ... to comment on the results of the report by the Royal Commission on the Newest Reproductive Technologies, which was released last—

(ROBERT, half asleep, hits the snooze button. ONEIDA dreams.)

INTERCOM: *(As in the hospital.)* And the prime minister is emerging now ... the prime minister.

(Separate on the stage, under bright lights, a very pregnant PRIME MINISTER steps up to a microphone. Behind her stands a BODYGUARD wearing shades, surreptitiously glancing over the audience and murmuring into his lapel walkie-talkie.)

PRIME MINISTER: It is no secret that our country is in the throes of an economic crisis. It has been determined that the cost of maintaining our social safety net far surpasses the tax base that our population is willing to provide for this system.

(Suddenly, her water breaks. She freezes. The BODYGUARD produces a towel and begins to mop it up off the ground and up her legs. She continues her address seemingly nonplussed.)

Consequently, Parliament has no alternative but to make items such as health care, education and employment available only to those who are most ... deserving.

(She has a contraction and uses a puffing breathing technique to get through it before continuing her address. The BODYGUARD mirrors her action slightly, as a birth attendant would. From here on the labour progresses at a ridiculous speed.)

As a means of ensuring a healthier population, able to substantially contribute to the federal treasury, new legislation has this afternoon been unanimously approved to counteract the destructive trend of negative reproduction.

(Another contraction. She grabs the BODYGUARD and motions to him to commence effleurage—stroking of the belly—as she speaks.)

All pregnant women will undergo an early prenatal examination, the purpose of which will be to determine genetic excellence of their offspring. Upon passing this examination, the unborn will receive a Liveability Licence.

(The PRIME MINISTER gets down on all-fours. The BODYGUARD adjusts the microphone for her. She hits the floor with her fists and angrily motions for him to apply deep pressure to her back.)

Failure to receive this licence will result in a recommendation for termination of the pregnancy. Should the parents in question due to religious or other beliefs, decide upon carrying an imperfect child to term, the child will become a ward of the soon-to-be-established Reserves.

(She gets up into a squatting position, supported by the BODY-GUARD.)

As a preventative measure, sterilization of the infant will ensure that the undesirable traits in question will no longer affect future generations!

(The PRIME MINISTER heaves a mighty push.)

Ooooaahhh!

(Lights out on the PRIME MINISTER. ONEIDA bolts up, suddenly.)

ONEIDA: Holy sheesh!

ROBERT: *(Startled awake.)* What? What?

ONEIDA: Did you hear that?

ROBERT: What?

ONEIDA: ... New legislation ... is the radio on?

ROBERT: I pushed the snooze button.

ONEIDA: Before the news?

ROBERT: We got headlines—

ONEIDA: Did the Prime Minister come on?

ROBERT: I don't think so.

ONEIDA: Do we have a woman Prime Minister?

ROBERT: Not anymore.

ONEIDA: Oh. Okay. Never mind. Go back to sleep.

ROBERT: Too much adrenaline.

ONEIDA: I'm sorry.

ROBERT: No, no, it's a refreshing way to start the day.

(Pause.)

ONEIDA: Weird.

ROBERT: What?

ONEIDA: A world where only "perfect" children are born. Everyone needs a "liveability licence." Imperfects would be sent to the "reserves." All these things I've been reading ... maybe it's not so far off—

ROBERT: Hm.

ONEIDA: You know, maybe it's not such a bad idea ... only healthy people ... I mean, what's so bad about that? Of course, you can't say that to anyone ... but—

ROBERT: Couldn't happen anyway.

ONEIDA: Why not?

ROBERT: It would put too many people out of work.

(He playfully attacks her. ONEIDA suddenly freezes.)

ONEIDA: Stop!

ROBERT: What's the matter?

ONEIDA: I get my test today.

(He kisses and holds her.

Separate on the stage, MAUREEN comes into view in tennis clothes and carrying her tennis racket. She has a portable phone in her hand. ONEIDA's phone rings. ROBERT picks it up.)

ROBERT: Yeah.

MAUREEN: Hello, is this Robert?

ROBERT: *(In an exotic accent.)* No, it's Oneida's lover.

ONEIDA: Robert—!

MAUREEN: Stranger things have happened. Is Oneida home?

(ONEIDA grabs the phone. ROBERT acts a fool, trying to make ONEIDA laugh.)

ONEIDA: Mom?

MAUREEN: Hello, darling. I can call you back if this is a bad time.

ONEIDA: No, it's fine.

MAUREEN: It's important to spend quality time with your husband. God knows, I should have been more patient with your father before he up and died like that.

ONEIDA: He didn't die, Mother. He moved to Pembroke with his accountant.

(ROBERT exits.)

MAUREEN: Pardon me?

ONEIDA: How are you?

MAUREEN: I'm excellent. Well?

ONEIDA: So far, okay.

MAUREEN: No bleeding?

ONEIDA: None. I go today for the test.

MAUREEN: Oh, good God.

ONEIDA: Mom—

MAUREEN: Oh, Oneida ... it's just ... when I see these pathetic women in the paper—after IVF—with three, four, five babies ... it makes me nervous. You know, one child is sufficient, two is ... tolerable I suppose, but any more than that and you can say goodbye to your life, Oneida. Perhaps even goodbye to your marriage. And then where will you be? Six children and no husband.

ONEIDA: They only put three in, it can't be any more than that.

MAUREEN: Well, I'm off to Westport for a match for a few days and, well ... We've never really had a good heart-to-heart about this ... I don't know why you feel you can't speak with me, have I not made you feel comfortable in confiding to me? Oh, never mind, I'll just come out and say it—

ONEIDA: What?

MAUREEN: You know, Oneida, being a mother isn't all it's cracked up to be.

ONEIDA: What do you mean?

MAUREEN: Even in the best of circumstances ... there are no guarantees that what you get is ... well ... what you had hoped for.

ONEIDA: Speaking as your only child I'm not sure how I should take that.

MAUREEN: Oneida, don't get me wrong, dear ... You know I want for you whatever will make you happy. You seem to think that having a baby is going to make you happy. And this is what I'm concerned about ...

(The dull "beep" of call-waiting is heard.)

Oh, would you hold, please?

(MAUREEN puts ONEIDA on hold. ONEIDA suddenly senses something between her legs. She puts her hands under her gown. When she pulls them out they are covered in blood. Re-enter ROBERT. She shakily holds her hands up to him. She begins to collapse with

sorrow. ROBERT picks her up and rocks her. MAUREEN comes back on the line.)

That was the club. There's a court free at eight, so I'll make this quick.

Happiness has to come from within you, darling. You can't expect someone else to bring it to you. You can't order it like a meal in a restaurant.

(ROBERT slowly carries her out of the room as MAUREEN continues.)

Happiness comes with personal pride. Enjoyment with what you do. Your career, your hobbies, your partner, politics, exercise, religion, even volunteer work, if you wish. All of these things can be beneficial and fulfilling, and most of all, can bring you happiness. And once you are capable yourself of attaining and maintaining happiness, then and only then should you be thinking of bringing a child into your life. A child to share in your happiness. Not provide you with it.

Oneida? Oneida? Damn these telephones ...

(MAUREEN is about to redial, but checks her watch and decides against it. She exits.

Visual: sperm forcing its way into an egg; cellular activity.)

Scene Six

(Dr. Krumm's examination room. ONEIDA lays on the examination table. DR. KRUMM and ROBERT stand beside it.)

DR. KRUMM: I strongly advise you against any further attempts. The results, or, lack of them I should say, clearly indicate that you are simply not a suitable candidate for IVF, Oneida. I am sorry. As I have suggested before, you can register with an adoption agency.

ROBERT: Ten years is too long to wait. We've already wasted seven years.

DR. KRUMM: There are many needy older children, who would greatly benefit from a home such as yours.

ROBERT: It's just not suitable for us. We don't want somebody else's problem.

DR. KRUMM: Then, I suggest you simply move on with your life. Take a break if you need it, a holiday maybe—

ROBERT: *(His anger rising.)* With what, "Doctor"? We've spent everything we've got on this scam! I can't even buy a baby off the black market, now!

DR. KRUMM: You were clearly made aware of the risks in the contract—

(ROBERT hits the desk with his fist.)

ROBERT: How the hell can this happen, man?!

DR. KRUMM: Mr. Kilborn—

ROBERT: A whole shitload of money!

ONEIDA: Robert—

ROBERT: I always thought—it can't happen to us—it can't happen to *me*—I've been a patient husband, a productive employee, a good neighbour, even! ... For Christ's sake! I have nothing, now!

ONEIDA: Robert—

ROBERT: All my friends have houses, Oneida. Houses, cottages, cars, children, RRSPs. I've got to start from fuckin' scratch again. From scratch! I'm forty years old! I've got nothing!

(DR. KRUMM clears his throat.)

DR. KRUMM: Surely, you take comfort in your marriage, Robert.

(ROBERT makes no response.)

These feelings of frustration are quite understandable. I can refer you to a counsellor, if you wish ... perhaps just for a while, to assist you in overcoming—

(ROBERT grabs DR. KRUMM by the collar and shoves him down on the table.)

ROBERT: We've been through all that shit with those idiot group sessions already! Fuck that idea. Fuck the whole thing!

(ROBERT exits.)

DR. KRUMM: Excuse me.

(DR. KRUMM exits after ROBERT. SISTER appears.)

SISTER: Wow.

ONEIDA: What the hell just happened, here?

SISTER: A little out of character, would you say?

ONEIDA: That wasn't Robert.

SISTER: It looked like Robert.

ONEIDA: Robert doesn't get violent.

SISTER: It looked like violence.

ONEIDA: Well, he's upset. He has a right to be. What he says is true ... we really don't have anything to show for everything we've ... spent.

SISTER: There's more than money at stake here, lady. Think of what you've gone through. All he had to do was jerk off!

ONEIDA: I haven't paid enough attention to him. It's always been about me. My aches. My pains. My anger. I should have been more ... less ... shit!

SISTER: Stop it now, you're being pathetic.

ONEIDA: That's how he really feels. It's been a waste. All that time with me has been a waste! He could have had a whole baseball team by now with someone else. I can't even squeak out a shortstop. *(Crying.)* Oh ... God ...

SISTER: Oh, 'Neidi. Okay ... okay ... shh ... shh ... look, so Robbie can't take the heat. Worst case scenario ...

ONEIDA: He leaves.

SISTER: Okay, so?

ONEIDA: I love him! I know it's a boring and outdated concept, to love one's husband, but I do!

SISTER: Well, then, I suppose you'll have to search for another means of attaining your objective.

ONEIDA: Like what?

SISTER: Surely, the good doctor must have some other ideas.

(DR. KRUMM re-enters. He places a twenty-dollar-bill on his desk.)

DR. KRUMM: Ah ... Robert gave me this to pass on to you. For a taxi.

ONEIDA: What did he say?

DR. KRUMM: Um ... he said ... he'll see you at home ... later.

ONEIDA: How much later?

DR. KRUMM: He wasn't clear on that point. *(He clears his throat.)* Infertility is an extremely emotional issue ... Of course, you already know that, but, in any event, should you, yourself need some further counselling, I know of several highly qualified—

ONEIDA: You know, Dr. Krumm, I've been reading a great deal about reproductive technology. Almost every day it seems, there's something new, somewhere—

DR. KRUMM: Yes.

ONEIDA: There's so much experimenting going on with new methods of conception—

DR. KRUMM: Uh huh.

ONEIDA: Sometimes using volunteers—

DR. KRUMM: Uh hm—

ONEIDA: Well, I thought that, maybe you know someone ... or ... some company ... who might be trying something different ... maybe something controversial, even ... behind closed doors ... or underground ... who could ... use ...

DR. KRUMM: You wish to be used as a human guinea pig?

ONEIDA: You know we don't have any more money—

DR. KRUMM: I'm afraid I can't—

ONEIDA: It's just not fair that people with money can keep trying ... all this new stuff ... making perfect babies ... Just because you're rich doesn't mean you'd be a good parent. It only means you'd have ... perfect, wealthy children!

DR. KRUMM: Oneida. Your husband is experiencing difficulty accepting our failure. He may blame me, himself, and even you, and sometimes he may act ... irrationally. But, I'm certain that it will pass, in time. And that your marriage, if it is a solid one based on—

ONEIDA: *(Interrupting.)* Are you married, Doctor Krumm?

DR. KRUMM: Me? Um. No. Actually, I'm ... divorced.

ONEIDA: I see.

DR. KRUMM: But don't take that to mean that I don't appreciate how a worthwhile relationship, such as yours and Robert's should operate. Not at all. I know. Believe me. I tried. Seven years I tried.

Partnership, understanding, mutual support, appreciation of individual ambition ... these are the mortar of a modern marriage. How about spontaneity? Practicality? Comprehension and acceptance of sporadic difficulties? For instance, the spouse's occasional, unwelcome *but necessary* need for additional time at work—say—toiling late nights in the laboratory—performing *ground-breaking research* that may *change the face* of medical technologies on this planet and put *one's own picture* on the cover of respected, international medical journals!

I did it for *us!* For *our future!!*

A mere forgotten birthday, or postponed vacation or two, need not result in a calamitous court duel where the defendant is forced to relinquish half—half!—of everything he owns and may acquire in the future—with no thanks to Mrs. "This Isn't a Marriage, Anymore"!

(He clears his throat and sits down and resumes his doctorly etiquette.)

A solid marriage should be based on the love you have for each other, grounded in reality. Not based on some dream that can't be actualized.

ONEIDA: Our dream involved a child or two. Nothing wild or extraordinary. Not fame or excess fortune. Just a child. If I can't produce that, I can't hold this marriage together.

DR. KRUMM: You shouldn't jump so quickly to negative—

ONEIDA: Look, Dr. Krumm, you must know something, someone ... some Dr. Frankenstein-type-guy fooling around with mice who's dying to get hold of a real, live, *human* womb!

DR. KRUMM: Even if I did know someone, I am bound by certain ethical codes which don't allow such flagrant disregard for humane principals. We don't live in a B-movie, here, Oneida.

ONEIDA: So, you're not going to help me.

DR. KRUMM: I have no more to offer. Now, if you'll excuse me I have another appointment—

ONEIDA: Fine. Fine. I'll do it myself, then. I'll find someone to help me.

DR. KRUMM: I have a very big problem with the idea of you spending your good time chasing a notion that most likely will end in more disappointment.

(ONEIDA moves in on him, eventually pushing him down on the desk as ROBERT did.)

ONEIDA: No. I don't think that's your problem at all. You don't want me to have success somewhere else, because it will make *you* look bad. I know the way this industry works. It's just one big competition for research grants. The hospital with the biggest statistics brings home the prize! Right?!

Well, let me tell you, Dr. Krumm, I'm more than a statistic on one of your stupid grant applications, I'm not just some ignorant, faceless receptacle! I'm—

Goodbye.

DR. KRUMM: Um ... Oneida ...

(She looks back. He holds up the twenty. She ignores him and exits with SISTER.

Visual: human egg dividing into four cells.)

Scene Seven

(The bedroom, that night. ONEIDA is reading a magazine in bed. She hears something. She puts her magazine down.)

ONEIDA: Robert?

(SISTER appears with a bottle of Tia Maria and two glasses.)

SISTER: He's probably just out drinking with the boys.

ONEIDA: Robert doesn't drink.

(SISTER pours the drinks.)

SISTER: Maybe he should. Cheers.

(They drink.)

What in God's name are you reading now? *Mondo 2000?*

ONEIDA: It's a cyberpunk magazine.

SISTER: Really?

ONEIDA: It's a cultural thing ... cyberpunk, cybernetics, cyberspace—

SISTER: Online computer heads who consider themselves philosophers of the electronic revolution.

ONEIDA: Right. The most I can gather is they wear funny looking clothes, communicate via Internet, decompose software—

SISTER: —and spout orations on the new order of love and intelligence.

ONEIDA: Yeah. A kind of a nineties answer to the sixties.

(She gets another drink and knocks it back.)

SISTER: And dare I ask, where did you get this magazine?

ONEIDA: Last week.

SISTER: I didn't ask when, I asked where.

(Pause.)

ONEIDA: In an arcade.

(SISTER begins to laugh.)

What's so funny?

SISTER: It's a far cry from *Chatelaine* and *Better Homes and Gardens.*

ONEIDA: I know.

SISTER: There's no law that says you can't change if you want to.

ONEIDA: I don't want to be a cyberpunk. There's some interesting articles in here, that's all.

At least, I think they are. I mean they probably would be if I could understand them ... All this computer—electronic stuff, everything's happening so quickly ... and the things they are saying that are going to be possible ...

I mean ... with our bodies even ... like ... we already are cyborgs—

SISTER: Cybernetic organisms.

ONEIDA: Yes. Anyone with a fake, functional body part, like a pace-maker, according to definition is, technically, a cyborg.

SISTER: Now that's interesting.

(A stumbling is heard off stage. The sound of ROBERT vomiting. ONEIDA and SISTER look to each other.)

ONEIDA: Maybe he should drink more often.

> *(ROBERT blindly stumbles into the room. He is a mess; his shirt is half off. He falls onto the bed. ONEIDA pokes him.)*

Robert.

> *(She pulls off his shirt. She holds the shirt in her hands studying the collar. SISTER moves close and studies the shirt with ONEIDA.)*

Max Factor?

SISTER: *(Shaking her head.)* Revlon.

ONEIDA: Well, I never said he had a great imagination.

> *(She smells the shirt, and holds it out to SISTER.)*

"Eternity"?

> *(SISTER takes the shirt and sniffs it.)*

SISTER: "Escape."

> *(A long pause as ONEIDA works to deny her internal rage.)*

ONEIDA: You know, a funny thing happened at the mall.

I went into that designer kids store. They had the most adorable bunting bags. I bought two, just in case, in size eighteen months; because, you know, what with all the growth hormones in our water table now, from the cows' excretions ... have you heard about this?

SISTER: Yes.

ONEIDA: Oh. Okay. So, then I was on my way to the bus stop, I pass by this arcade ...

> *(The bells and sonics of an arcade are heard, accompanied by flashing and strobing multicoloured lights.)*

I've never been into one of these before, and I think to myself, I better get hip because I don't want to be one of those technologically illiterate parents, I want to share these experiences with my children.

SISTER: Uh huh.

ONEIDA: In the middle of the arcade is one of these Virtual Reality set-ups. "Inner Space," it's called ...

> *(Effects add to ONEIDA's memory.)*

I climb into it, put the glove on, put the helmet on ... Man, this thing ... you're like, right in it ... like totally ... it's the coolest, most far-out experience! Snipers shooting at you, and space ships with lasers ... like you get killed continually but you never get hurt ...!

> *(Pause.)*

And then I realize that this technology has greater possibilities. If one was to modify this machine, and exercise the proper synapses, it could actually be used as a Virtual Pregnancy Monitor. To be used when one has been Invirtually Fertilized. Because this is the way of the future. And the future is now!

With a Virtual Pregnancy Monitor we could see, feel, hear ... experience *all* of our wombial activity. The true "inner space." We ... could ... connect. We could nurture, inform and educate our babies, prebirth! Do you understand what this means? *A whole new generation* of genetically engineered embryos ... cyberwomb gestation! The intellectually and psychologically strengthening ramifications in the newborn will be astounding!

And *we* are going to *be* amongst the *lucky pioneers* of *Dr. Spock's new frontier!!*

(Pause.)

SISTER: I'll go put this in the wash.

(Exit SISTER with the shirt.

The PRIME MINISTER's previous address is heard in electronically treated bits and pieces as the scene is prepared for ONEIDA's Invirtual Fertilization dream.)

PRIME MINISTER: *(Voiceover.)* Social safety net ... available only to those who are most ... deserving ... to counter-act the destructive trend of negative reproduction ... the unborn will receive a Liveability Licence ... an imperfect child will become a ward of the soon-to-be-established Reserves.

(DR. KRUMM and two pregnant NURSES appear ready for surgery. The dialogue is electronically enhanced and comes from somewhere other than their mouths.)

ONEIDA: Dr. Krumm, why didn't you tell me about this before—

DR. KRUMM: I have to be very careful. Everyone is watching everyone.

ONEIDA: Don't I have to sign something?

DR. KRUMM: No paper trails.

NURSE: Deep breath.

(ONEIDA draws in a breath, a NURSE administers a needle.)

ONEIDA: I am given chemical relaxants. Doctor Krumm assures me that these chemicals are in no way harmful to me, or my soon-to-be-conceived babies. We have agreed upon twins, as we may not be able to do this more than once. My body and my mind must exist at the peak of susceptibility.

I am conceptually susceptible.

(Possible image: DR. KRUMM works behind a sheet which is held up by the NURSES. We see him operating a cyber-glove, similar to a virtual reality glove. ONEIDA kneels in front of the sheet.)

I wait for the familiar drill, or the poke or the tweak of some none-too-distant painful procedure, but I feel nothing. They assure me it is not because I am frozen, but because this method is not such that requires the crude utensils of in vitro fertilization gone past. This is a cyber-system of embryo construction. One that is completely painless.

They ask me which sense-memory tape I would like to play, while they tend to the physical details.

I choose "The Night of the Laughing Orgasm."

Unlike other orgasms, often accompanied by the uncontrollable release of sadness and tears, this night is different ...

As the sensation increases—that unmistakable assurance that all is well, and indeed this is going to be one of those rare, lucky times—a faint and funny tickling under the ribs coincides with my pelvic eruptions. *(She begins to giggle.)* I am overwhelmed with glee and burst into spontaneous laughter *(She laughs uproariously.)* which is both surprising and confusing to Robert, *(Laughing still.)* but pleasing nonetheless.

(She sighs contentedly.)

The doctor removes the cyber-system devices of invirtual fertilization. The first phase of conception is complete.

(Exit DR. KRUMM and the NURSES.)

We must now await the verdict, of which, I am certain, is this time, to be positive.

Scene Eight

(The bedroom, a few weeks later. ONEIDA is sitting cross-legged, performing her kegels, a vaginal exercise designed to strengthen the birth canal. SISTER is holding an instructional booklet and counting for her.)

SISTER: One, two, three, hold. *(Pause.)* One, two, three, release. Good. How many times was he out this week?

ONEIDA: I don't know, two or three—

SISTER: You're just going to let it go on?

ONEIDA: I haven't figured it out yet.

SISTER: Now in five ... One, two, three, four—

ONEIDA: *(Interrupting.)* Five? Let me see that.

(ONEIDA looks in the book.)

SISTER: What is there to figure out?

ONEIDA: How the hell can I contract to the count of five ... what do they think I am ... Robovaj?

SISTER: You have enough evidence. Lipstick, perfume, late nights ... You have to confront him with it. *(Beat.)* Information is power.

ONEIDA: What's to stop him from turning and running?

(Pause.)

SISTER: Did you throw up again this morning?

(Pause.)

ONEIDA: All my breakfast, and part of last night's dinner.

(They look at each other.)

SISTER: Bingo.

(ROBERT enters with a parcel.)

ONEIDA: Hi!

ROBERT: Hi.

ONEIDA: Did you have a good day?

ROBERT: What constitutes a good day, Oneida? Is payday a good day? How can it possibly be, when practically all your pay-cheque is devoured by an automatic withdrawal to pay the rent on a run-down garden home that doesn't even have a garden and you don't own anyway!

ONEIDA: Is that for me?

(ROBERT hands her the package, which she opens.)

ROBERT: Is Friday a good day? How can it be, when it's followed by two endless days with nothing to do, nowhere to go, and no one to see? Oh, maybe we could rent a movie, but the VCR is broken. And who wants a Hollywood ending anyway? It's like pulling a yellow highlighter through the shittiness of our own goddamn life.

ONEIDA: Look. *The ABCs of Breastfeeding.*

ROBERT: I thought we decided you were going to cancel your membership to the Parenting Book Club.

ONEIDA: I decided that would be foolish. I only have to order two more books to get a free one.

ROBERT: What the hell for!

ONEIDA: I'm saving for the *Newborn Medical Encyclopedia.* It's a fifty-four dollar value, you know.

ROBERT: It's not going to happen. Why do you keep torturing yourself like this?

ONEIDA: This isn't torture. I'm getting stronger everyday. Maybe if you'd make love to me once in a while you'd notice the difference.

ROBERT: You're the one who didn't want to have sex any more.

(ROBERT exits.)

SISTER: That was your cue.

ONEIDA: I don't think now is a good time.

SISTER: You can't continue—

ONEIDA: Now is not a good time!

SISTER: Why not?

(ROBERT re-enters holding a box containing the disassembled guts of a computer.)

ROBERT: *(Controlled.)* What happened to the computer?

ONEIDA: I took it apart.

SISTER: Not a good time.

ROBERT: *(Not understanding.)* Took it apart—

ONEIDA: I wanted to see how it worked.

ROBERT: Took ... it ... apart.

ONEIDA: With that little screwdriver from my sewing machine kit.

ROBERT: *Took ... it ... apart!!*

ONEIDA: Yes!

ROBERT: For Christ's sake! Do you know how to put it back together again?

SISTER: You know ...

ONEIDA: It's amazing all the stuff inside there ... you would never guess—

SISTER: I think maybe ...

ROBERT: Are you *nuts?!*

ONEIDA: All those little pieces can carry so much information—

SISTER: Now would be a good time—

ROBERT: I have things in here that I need! My work!

SISTER: You could change the subject.

ONEIDA: Right. I need to ask you something, Robert.

ROBERT: —files—

ONEIDA: This is important!

ROBERT: Data! I don't believe this! I've got to get out of here.

(ROBERT moves to exit. ONEIDA stops him.)

ONEIDA: I really *need* to know!

ROBERT: All right. Fuck. What difference does it make? Ask me. Come on, ask me. I'll tell you, goddamnit. I'll tell you whatever you want to know.

(ONEIDA searches his face carefully.)

Ask me!!

(Pause. She swallows.)

ONEIDA: *(Seriously.)* Would you love me twice as much if we had twins?

(ROBERT stares at her blankly, then turns to exit.)

Where are you going?

ROBERT: Crazy.

(Exit ROBERT.)

ONEIDA: *(To SISTER.)* Shut up.

SISTER: I didn't say anything.

ONEIDA: Don't you get it? The day he tells me is the day he's out of here. And then what? Look at the statistics. Welcome to the nineties ... Sister.

SISTER: I know it doesn't—

ONEIDA: No, you don't. You don't know anything. As a matter of fact, I am totally fed up with you constantly butting in!

SISTER: You wanted me here.

ONEIDA: You're a nuisance!

SISTER: You hated being an only child.

ONEIDA: That's why Mother terminated you.

SISTER: You think she wanted you?

ONEIDA: Shut up!

SISTER: The only reason you're here and I'm not is timing. The only thing you were good for was Dad's campaign photograph.

ONEIDA: *Beat it!!*

SISTER: But he left, anyway. Didn't he?

(SISTER leaves. ONEIDA takes pieces of the computer in her hands and studies them, an idea forming. A phone rings. MAUREEN emerges wearing English riding pants and a hard hat and carrying a crop. The answering machine clicks on.)

MACHINE: Hi. You've reached Robert and Oneida's house ... you know the drill.

> *(Beep.)*

MAUREEN: This is your mother, Oneida. I was just wondering how you're enjoying being back at the office. You know, a social life can bring rewards of friendship, which can last a lifetime. Do you have a social life, Oneida? Perhaps you ought to think about making some friends. Anyway, I have shows for the next few weekends, but, I might be free around the fifteenth. Perhaps we should pencil in lunch, hm?

> *(ONEIDA holds a cable which she tentatively places against her head.)*

I'll call you closer to then.

ONEIDA: Break a leg.

> *(ONEIDA carries off the box.*
>
> *The sound of a crying baby continues into the next scene.)*

Scene Nine

> *(Cindy's house—the baby's room. CINDY is tiredly tucking a baby to sleep in a decorated bassinet. The baby stops crying. ONEIDA peeks around the corner.)*

ONEIDA: Hi, Cindy.

CINDY: Oneida—

ONEIDA: I guess my invitation got lost in the mail. I heard about it at work. I didn't want to miss a friend's baby shower.

CINDY: Actually, I ... just thought you probably wouldn't want to come.

ONEIDA: You mean you didn't invite me?

CINDY: To tell you the truth ... I figured the last place you'd want to be is around someone who's just had a baby.

ONEIDA: Well, that's stupid.

> *(Pause.)*

CINDY: Would you like some punch? There's some in the kitchen.

ONEIDA: So, I guess that's her, huh?

CINDY: Yes. This is Angela.

ONEIDA: Awww.

CINDY: Just put her down for her nap.

ONEIDA: Well here, I brought her a present.

CINDY: Oh, thank you ...

*(ONEIDA pulls a little pair of unwrapped gloves out of her pocket.
One one of them there is an extra finger crudely sewn on in a
different colour.)*

CINDY: *(Confused.)* Little gloves—

ONEIDA: I sewed the extra finger on myself. You know, I looked all over
town, there simply is no place to get a six-fingered, left-handed baby
glove.

CINDY: I suppose that would be difficult.

ONEIDA: So, what are you planning to do about that hand, anyway?

CINDY: Uh ... I ... we think we're going to have the extra digit surgically
removed. It's a very simple procedure.

ONEIDA: Oooh, I don't know.

CINDY: I've talked to three different surgeons, they assure me that—

ONEIDA: Oh, no it's not that, I'm sure they'll lop it off just fine ... it's
just—

CINDY: What?

ONEIDA: Well, you might want to play your cards ... carefully.

CINDY: What cards?

ONEIDA: Are you planning to do this through your medical coverage?

CINDY: Well, yes, otherwise it'll be unaffordable.

ONEIDA: Not a good idea.

CINDY: Why not?

ONEIDA: Cindy, I consider you a friend ... and I just wouldn't want to see
anything bad happen—

CINDY: What are you talking about?

ONEIDA: I know this may sound a little wild, but, I have reason to believe
that we're headed towards a reproductive police state.

CINDY: Police state?

ONEIDA: We are driving in the fast lane towards a society of zero
tolerance.

CINDY: What does this have to do with Angela?

ONEIDA: I don't mean to be impertinent ... but basically what you have
here is a genetic "imperfect."

CINDY: Pardon me?

ONEIDA: Even if you chop off that extra digit, she still is going to carry
that degenerate gene. And the way genes work ... who knows? You

may be in store for a two-headed grandson. They're just not going to let that happen.

CINDY: "They" who?

ONEIDA: The government, of course. They can't afford it any more. Angie would be targeted.

CINDY: Targeted for what?

ONEIDA: It's all coming down, Cindy. Mandatory prenatal testing ... Liveability Licences ... Reserves for Imperfects—

CINDY: Jesus, Oneida—

ONEIDA: My advice: Get the surgery done privately ... no paper trails ... that way, she'll have a better chance.

CINDY: Oneida, I'm sorry, I'm going to have ask you to leave.

ONEIDA: You're kicking me out of a baby shower?

CINDY: I know you've suffered, but I don't appreciate you coming over here with inappropriate gifts and saying rude things like that.

ONEIDA: Rude? This isn't rude. This may very well be reality! I'm trying to help.

CINDY: Well, you're not.

ONEIDA: Oh, and I suppose downstairs they are. Tell me ... did anyone even mention Angie's deformity? I bet not. I bet they all did their polite best not to notice that extra pinky. And I bet you even pulled the little hand cover over on her nightie, didn't you? So that when they held her they wouldn't have to look at it ...

(ONEIDA looks in the basinet.)

Let me see ... are you trying to pretend it doesn't exist?

CINDY: Please, Oneida ... I just got her to sleep.

ONEIDA: You did ... you're trying to cover it up!

CINDY: I'm trying to keep her warm!

ONEIDA: Hiding from the problem is going to get you nowhere! The only way you can protect her is to take things into your own hands, find your own solutions and beat the bastards at their own game!

CINDY: Angela's problem is very likely caused by some environmental thing ... man-made carpets, radioactive waves, synthetic hormones in the water table—

ONEIDA: It doesn't matter how it got there! Your job is to deal with it now, for the future, and the first thing you've got to do is admit to yourself that your child is a mutant!

CINDY: My child is not a mutant.

ONEIDA: Yes, she is.

CINDY: No, she's not!

ONEIDA: I'm sorry, but by definition, Angela is a bona fide mutant!

CINDY: Who do you think you are! ... Taking your envy out on me, just because you can't have a baby! You're the one who's got something wrong—something really wrong ... something *big time* wrong! *You're* the mutant, lady! That's right! You're the mutant! Degenerate! *Monster!! Freak!!*

> *(The baby begins crying again. CINDY picks it up and begins to jostle it.)*

Oh, my god! Look how you've made me act! I've never called anyone names before. This is your fault! And now you've woken up the baby ... and I haven't slept for seventy-eight hours and my breasts are leaking like a garden hose! Get out! Get out of my house now!

ONEIDA: *(Calmly.)* While we're seeking for the truth, you might as well know everything. Information is power after all. Your husband is banging Betty Boop in Customer Service and everybody knows but you.

CINDY: You're demented.

ONEIDA: Go on. I dare you. Go downstairs and listen really closely. You're bound to hear something sooner or later. All that time you were sweating and barfing while you grew that mutant for the both of you, he was porking his brains out with Little Miss Titsy-Butt.

> *(CINDY is speechless. ONEIDA turns to leave then looks back at her and raises her fist high in the air.)*

Feel the power.

> *(She exits.*
>
> *Visual: an early stage embryo.)*

Scene Ten

(The bedroom, one week later.)

ONEIDA: *(Voiceover.)* Before an Olympic skier lunges through the gate, she visualizes. She skis the course in her mind. From beginning to end. A flawless run, a winning time. It is an effective mental exercise proven to enhance the athlete's confidence and thus her performance.

> *(ONEIDA is donning a strange-looking apparatus, which she has obviously made herself, fashioned from various kitchen utensils and computer components. It suggests a combination of a virtual reality helmet and a fetal heart-rate monitor. The headpiece consists of a makeshift eyecover, earphones, microphone, and a cable reaching to*

a belt. The wide, elasticized abdomenal belt has on it a connector into which the cable can be attached. She also has a glove—a modified, industrial rubber one, on which there are glued several computer chips and wires. It should be similar to the one DR. KRUMM used in the Invirtual Fertilization scene. After she is hooked up, she stands with her hands on her abdomen, deep in thought.)

Six weeks. Formation of the head, chest and abdominal cavities. Development of rudimentary brain, spinal column and proper spinal chord. Disappearance of fetal tail, appearance of limb buds. Formation of heart, simple circulation. Face unshapen. Small depressions indicate situation of eyes and ears. Total length, six millimetres.

Times two.

One boy and one girl.

(Enter ROBERT. He warily observes her.)

ROBERT: Oneida?

ONEIDA: You're home early.

ROBERT: What the hell is that?

ONEIDA: You mean this old thing?

ROBERT: You've got pieces of my ... what is this?

ONEIDA: It's a Virtual Pregnancy Monitor.

ROBERT: A Virtual Pregnancy Monitor.

ONEIDA: I made it myself. You should admire my thriftiness.

ROBERT: Jesus Christ.

ONEIDA: It allows you to communicate with your baby in utero. You must only think happy thoughts. Only ... I have to think them ... times two ... for twins. So I'm twice as happy.

ROBERT: You're joking, right?

ONEIDA: No, I'm very serious. All the material supports it. Happiness starts in the womb, dear. *(Pause.)* I wanted to wait to tell you until it was more obvious but ... Here, you try it—

ROBERT: No.

ONEIDA: I know it's going to take a while to sink in ... all those "wasted" years with no results ...but finally ... the marvel of science has made us the happy parents of twins! You see, we are an integral part of a new secret project. You mustn't tell anyone yet. They still have to do the test, but ... I have a really good feeling about this. Come on ... say hello to Michael and Chrissy.

ROBERT: Michael and Chrissy.

ONEIDA: Well, you'd pick ordinary names too, if your name was "Oneida."

ROBERT: Look, would you just quit fucking around!

ONEIDA: Please, Robert watch your language around the children.

(ROBERT is silent. ONEIDA giggles.)

Oh, Robert ... of course I'm joking. *(Pause.)* Oh, c'mon, you think I'd really ... *(Pause.)* Stop looking at me like that ... It was just something to do.

ROBERT: Oneida, I have to talk to you. Sit down.

(She moves to sit.)

No ... take that thing off, first.

ONEIDA: Okay, but you are interrupting an important happy thought session.

ROBERT: *Just* ... listen.

ONEIDA: You didn't lose your job, did you?

ROBERT: No.

ONEIDA: Of course not. I mean, how could they fire you ... all those nights you've been working late.

(Pause.)

ROBERT: You know, don't you?

ONEIDA: Know what?

ROBERT: Don't you want to know about it?

ONEIDA: Know about what?

ROBERT: The woman I've been seeing.

ONEIDA: Not particularly.

ROBERT: We met at a computer networking seminar. Last fall.

(Pause.)

Did you hear me, Oneida? Last fall. *(Pause.)* Last *fall. (Pause.) Last* fall. While we were going through the IVF! *(Pause.)* All the time we were trying to impregnate you I was sleeping with another woman! *(Pause.) Hello!!*

ONEIDA: And now she's pregnant.

ROBERT: Why do you say that?

ONEIDA: Why else would you be telling me now?

ROBERT: Yes.

ONEIDA: This is so bizarre. This is like the old days ... you know, when there were lots of babies to adopt ... and people who gave up trying to conceive would adopt one, and as soon as they did, they'd get pregnant ... so they'd end up suddenly with two, instead of one?

ROBERT: What does that have to do with it?

ONEIDA: I'm talking about the solution to your dilemma, Robert. Obviously, being the decent man that you are, you are torn ... confused about your responsibilities.

ROBERT: Well, yes, but—

ONEIDA: It's very simple. She can give the baby to us!

ROBERT: Oneida—

ONEIDA: I mean, what's the difference? Okay, okay ... her egg and her uterus. But it was your sperm, right? And you're my husband, and what's yours is mine, the law says so.

ROBERT: Oneida—

ONEIDA: We should be able to reach some sort of agreement, don't you think? I mean, she must be nice, otherwise you wouldn't be sleeping with her, right? We could give her money while she carries the child ... I know it's illegal but we'll pay cash. And I could coach her labour, I've read all about it. And then we'll have three! The whole she-bang in under a year!

ROBERT: Oneida ... don't start this again—

ONEIDA: *(Interrupting.)* Of course, it may be difficult to love it as much as our own ... But there is counselling for this sort of thing. I'm sure we can work it out. Already I feel a warmth towards the *bastard!*

ROBERT: Oneida—

ONEIDA: Just one thing, has it had its liveability examination? Because I wouldn't want to unknowingly adopt an imperfect and then have it whisked off to the Reserves ... That would kind of defeat the purpose, wouldn't it?

ROBERT: I'm moving in with her.

  (Pause.)

ONEIDA: As a matter of fact, I can use this device.

ROBERT: What—

ONEIDA: Sure! I can attach the uteral monitor to her and I wear the headpiece—

ROBERT: My God—

ONEIDA: I send the baby the messages ... it will know my voice, my electronic impulses!

ROBERT: *Oneida!!*

ONEIDA: It will never know the difference!

(He grabs the Virtual Pregnancy Monitor.)

ROBERT: This is not a Virtual Pregnancy Monitor! There are no Reserves for Imperfects! There is no such thing as a Liveability Licence!

(He throws it.)

ONEIDA: I know it's a difficult thing to accept, Robert, but so was the Goods and Services Tax. Just give it time. And then who knows ... in two or three years ... they'll give it another name. Like ... a Procreation Permit or a Gestation Authorization!

(ROBERT hits her.)

ROBERT: Shut up! Just shut the fuck up!

(She stands, stunned, shaking, staring wide-eyed at him.)

Oh, God ... Oneida ... I'm sorry ... please ... I'm so sorry.

(He goes to her. She emits a ferocious scream and starts to kick and pummel him. He protects himself but does not fight back. When she stops, she paces, trying to catch her breath, using small arm-flexing movements as in the top of scene one to regain calm.)

You got it straight now? I am in love with another woman. We are having a baby. I am going to be the father and she is going to be the mother. Not you.

(Exit ROBERT. Pause.)

ONEIDA: Go on. Go and sleep with your pregnant slut.

(She reaches for the Virtual Pregnancy Monitor.)

I can do it without you, now.

(End of Act One.)

Act Two

Scene One

(Oneida's garage, five weeks later.

In the dark—a lighter is lit, and used to ignite a blow-torch. Wearing a welding helmet and protective leather apron, ONEIDA passes the flame over a twelve-inch square piece of copper. After it is warmed, she turns off the torch. She lifts the visor, and begins to hammer the copper.

SISTER, now dressed more in cyber-wear, is seated in a corner, filing her nails with a metal file.)

SISTER: Did you file it first?

ONEIDA: So now you're a metalworking expert?

SISTER: The edge is very sharp. A cut may become infected. Infection is carried through the bloodstream. Your body will become most inhospitable.

(ONEIDA holds her hand out for the file.)

Truce, okay? None of it matters anymore. I can help you.

(ONEIDA nods. She begins to file the edge. MAUREEN calls from offstage.)

MAUREEN: Oneida!?

SISTER: Don't look now, but she's making a live appearance.

(ONEIDA removes her helmet. MAUREEN enters, finely dressed.)

ONEIDA: In person?

MAUREEN: I've always admired your dramatic element, 'Neidi. You know, had you not married Bobo the Clown, you might have done something with it.

(MAUREEN kisses her perfunctorily.)

How is my baby? Hm? Did you straighten out all the nasty business with the lawyer?

ONEIDA: *(Brightly.)* I got his tools!

79

MAUREEN: Well, you could always sell them, I suppose.

You know, when I divorced Randal, I managed to get his bloody coin collection ... remember? His paternal grandfather had started in goddamn 1842, or something like that. Well, I turned around and sold it for five thousand dollars! He was so angry! It was a lovely sight!

Oh! Metallurgical Sculpture! Oneida, I'm impressed! What a fitting outlet for you! You know, you could get onto the artsy scene. Galleries, parks, shopping malls ... you're bound to meet interesting people that way. This is exactly what I've been getting at. There is nothing like a creative endeavour to fill a void. Good for you, sweetheart. What are you calling this piece?

(ONEIDA looks to SISTER, then to MAUREEN.)

ONEIDA: Cyberwomb.

(Pause.)

MAUREEN: Well. I won't pretend to understand, I think it's better that way.

ONEIDA: What are you doing in town?

MAUREEN: *(Coyly.)* I have a lunch date.

ONEIDA: Really? With who?

MAUREEN: Someone I met at the gym.

ONEIDA: That's great, Mom. I'm happy for you. What's his name?

MAUREEN: Virginia.

ONEIDA: Oh.

MAUREEN: Our world is changing, Oneida. The old ways don't always work any more.

ONEIDA: No kidding.

MAUREEN: Do you mind if I watch? I have a few minutes to kill yet. I won't bother you.

ONEIDA: Oh, no ... sure.

(ONEIDA begins hammering again. SISTER bursts into laughter.)

SISTER: Virginia!

ONEIDA: You shouldn't be so hard on her.

SISTER: I have my reasons.

ONEIDA: Life with Dad wasn't exactly what she bargained for.

SISTER: Oh, but the papers loved it at the beginning, didn't they? "Olympic Bronze Medallist marries member of Provincial Parliament." Everything was hunky-dory until he decided to go federal.

MAUREEN: Oneida, do you sometimes find it hard to feel human?

ONEIDA: I don't understand what you mean.

MAUREEN: Have you, at any time, not felt the way everyone told you you were supposed to feel?

ONEIDA: I don't know. Why?

MAUREEN: I've never been interested in volunteer work. And lately, many of the women I know are taking up these "causes." Causes that I don't give a damn about, and can't imagine that I ever will. It's a ridiculous expectation, really, just because one is a middle-aged, white and female that one should feel obligated to knock on the doors of strangers and beg for money.

What do you think of that?

ONEIDA: That's your prerogative, I guess.

MAUREEN: You're absolutely right, Oneida. I don't owe anybody anything. Thank you. You've made me feel much better. Well, keep up the good work, 'Neidi. Remember, I'm always here for you.

(MAUREEN kisses her.)

Bye, Honey.

(Exit MAUREEN. ONEIDA watches her sadly as she goes.)

ONEIDA: Bye.

(SISTER moves behind ONEIDA and gently places her hand on ONEIDA's stomach.)

SISTER: The embryo, prior to the development of a nervous system, exists in a state of emotional symbiosis with its mother.

ONEIDA: The mother's thoughts are its thoughts.

SISTER: Feelings are passed like food through the placenta.

(ONEIDA places her hand over SISTER's.)

ONEIDA: Eleven weeks: fetus recognizable as a small human baby.

SISTER: Head appears relatively large for body, and limbs short, small and thin as few muscles have yet developed.

ONEIDA: Eyes completely formed, external ear continues to enlarge and assume adult shape. Fingers and toes still joined together.

SISTER: Movements of limb and spine increase. Heart functional and blood circulating to all parts of the body.

ONEIDA: Approximate length: five point five centimetres. Weight: ten grams.

SISTER: Times two.

(Sound: several newborns crying.)

Scene Two

(The hospital infant nursery, two weeks later. ONEIDA is peering into the infant nursery window. DR. KRUMM walks by.)

DR. KRUMM: Mrs. Kilborn ...?

ONEIDA: Dr. Krumm! I see your name on a number of the newborns in there. Congratulations.

DR. KRUMM: Do you know someone who's had a baby ...?

ONEIDA: Oh, no ... I was just looking ... killing time before my prenatal class movie.

DR. KRUMM: Well ... visiting hours are between four and eight ... and if you don't really have any connections to a family ... hospital policy, you understand. I'll walk you to the elevator.

ONEIDA: Actually, I'm glad I ran into you. I have good news.

DR. KRUMM: What's that?

ONEIDA: It worked.

DR. KRUMM: What worked?

ONEIDA: Swelling of the breasts, weight gain, nausea ... and I've missed two periods—

DR. KRUMM: I don't think we should be getting too excited—

ONEIDA: Why not?

DR. KRUMM: Oneida, in my opinion, I fear you may—

(A NURSE interrupts them.)

NURSE: Excuse me, Dr. Krumm ... haemorrhaging in 308—

DR. KRUMM: Okay ... Oneida ... If you would please make an appointment with my receptionist, we'll talk about this.

ONEIDA: Yes, okay ... and I think I should come in anyway for the test!

DR. KRUMM: Which test is that?

ONEIDA: *(Hushed.)* For their Liveability Licence!

(DR. KRUMM walks off, making a note on his clipboard.)

Scene Three

(Hospital Auditorium.

A film is running of a woman in the pushing stage of labour. ONEIDA is mesmerized by what she sees on the screen.

She becomes part of a scene whereby her cyber-delivery is enacted. The characters are herself, ROBERT, DR. KRUMM, and two pregnant NURSES. DR. KRUMM and the NURSES are in extreme cyber-wear.

Possible image: she wears a gown. Standing on the gurney, her arms and legs stretched spread eagle. DR. KRUMM controls the scene with his cyber-glove. ROBERT is puffing a cigar. The doctor passes the glove over her abdomen. He checks the readout. Dialogue can be voice-over as before.)

DR. KRUMM: Nine point seven five centimetres dilated. You're very nearly there, Mrs. Kilborn.

(ONEIDA groans in pain.)

ROBERT: I'm right here, babe.

ONEIDA: *(Painfully.)* What—what the hell is he doing here!?

DR. KRUMM: Hospital policy, Mrs. Kilborn.

ONEIDA: But ... he had nothing to do with it—he—it was all my—

DR. KRUMM: Hysterical hallucinatory malfunction ... Increase pleasure stimuli, nurses!

ONEIDA: Oh ... Ooooh ... *Ooohhhh!!*

(The NURSES inject her many times with sedatives and strap her to the gurney.)

Wait! Wait! Where are my babies. Where are my babies? They need me! Bring them to me right now! Michael! Chrissy! Don't cry! Mommy's coming!

Scene Four

(A hospital corridor in the psych ward. ONEIDA wakes on the gurney. Enter DR. EPSON, with a freaky cyber-head. DR. EPSON is gently proficient.)

DR. EPSON: Hello, Oneida. I'm Doctor Margaret Epson. I'm sorry you're out in the hall here ... but we're overflowing ... I'm just going to have a little look at your eyes ...

(ONEIDA reaches up to touch DR. EPSON's head. She is a little wary of her.)

The effects of the sedation will wear off shortly. How are you feeling, otherwise?

ONEIDA: Where's Dr. Krumm?

DR. EPSON: Dr. Krumm is on the third floor. This is the fifth. I am a psychiatrist.

ONEIDA: Well, what I need is an obstetrician.

DR. EPSON: Yes ... Dr. Krumm gave me some information.

ONEIDA: He did?

DR. EPSON: What you are experiencing, Oneida, is pseudocyesis. In layperson's terms ... an "hysterical, phantom or false pregnancy." It's a condition in which a woman has all the symptoms of pregnancy, but is actually not.

It usually afflicts women who intensely desire to be pregnant, but have failed to conceive. Judging from your records, your several attempts at IVF, it comes as no surprise, really. Certainly nothing to feel guilty about.

(ONEIDA strugles to sit up. SISTER appears and sits back to back with her, supporting ONEIDA.)

ONEIDA: Look at me, Doctor Epson. Look at my stomach! I normally have a very flat stomach.

DR. EPSON: Yes ... psychosomatic abdominal extension is not unheard of.

ONEIDA: Look, all I need is the test and then I can go.

DR. EPSON: You mean a pregnancy test?

ONEIDA: No ... I mean ... yes, actually.

DR. EPSON: We did perform a pregnancy test and it has come back negative.

ONEIDA: Oh, but those things, you can never be sure.

DR. EPSON: I can assure you they are quite accurate nowadays.

SISTER: Ask her.

ONEIDA: Was it a "regular" pregnancy test?

DR. EPSON: Yes. The same kind the hospital gives to everybody.

ONEIDA: Oh, I see.

SISTER: Well, that explains it then.

(DR. EPSON massages her own pregnant belly.)

DR. EPSON: As the time goes by, and your "pregnancy" does not continue to manifest itself in ways which are normal—most notably, further abdominal extension and failure to feel the baby move—you'll be able to more readily come to terms with it.

This kind of disorder responds favourably to a simple drug treatment for depression. You'll be feeling functional in no time.

ONEIDA: Can I go home now, then?

DR. EPSON: Do you feel you would be better off there?

ONEIDA: I don't see why I should be taking up valuable bed space.

DR. EPSON: Well, I don't believe you are a danger to either yourself, or anyone else. I'll see to your release right away.

Oh, we didn't find a name of anyone as an emergency contact for you in your personal belongings ... Is there anyone I can call for you?

(SISTER shakes her head.)

ONEIDA: No.

DR. EPSON: All right, then.

(Exit DR. EPSON.)

SISTER: Of course it isn't going to show up in a regular pregnancy test.

ONEIDA: They have no idea what they're dealing with.

(SISTER helps ONEIDA up.)

SISTER: You can't afford to slip like that again. Secrecy, remember? Krumm is not going to come out in the open about it. They could take his licence away ... or worse ... there's big bucks involved in this stuff, you know.

ONEIDA: I looks like we're on our own.

SISTER: Don't worry about it. Everything is under control.

(SISTER helps ONEIDA to walk out.)

Scene Five

(A grocery superstore, one week later. ONEIDA is pushing a shopping cart. ROBERT and DIANE are as well. Coming around the same corner, they collide.)

ROBERT: Hey!

DIANE: Excuse me!

(Pause.)

ONEIDA: Robert—

ROBERT: Oh, Christ—

ONEIDA: Imagine meeting you at the East End Super Clearance Food and Drug Warehouse Centre.

ROBERT: Why are you shopping in the East end?

ONEIDA: The flyer, of course. Hi, there! You must be Robert's new concubine.

ROBERT: Oneida—

DIANE: His fiancée, actually. My name is Diane.

ONEIDA: Fiancée. Diane. Well, isn't that nice. Die-ane. How is the gestation going?

DIANE: Fine.

ONEIDA: Six months is it?

DIANE: Almost.

ONEIDA: Can I feel it?

ROBERT: No, Oneida, you can't.

ONEIDA: I'm not talking to you, am I? Die-ane do you mind?

ROBERT: Come on—

DIANE: I can handle this, Rob. I'm sorry, Oneida, but I don't feel comfortable with the idea of you touching my body.

ONEIDA: All I'm asking for is a little feel. I'm not begging you to make me godmother or any such nonsense.

ROBERT: Let's go.

ONEIDA: Now, wait just a minute—"Rob"—let me attempt to appeal to your sense of logic, Diane.

ROBERT: There's no point in listening, believe me.

DIANE: Rob, why don't you give us a few minutes alone, hm?

   (ROBERT exits.)

   All right, Oneida. Say your piece.

ONEIDA: Here is me … plain in every respect. The jilted, pathetic, washed-up, ex-wife.

   There is you. Stunning, if I may be so forward. A simple seduction of a married man has swimmingly led you into perhaps a life-long commitment, stability, and a little bundle you can call your own. Now, tell me if I'm wrong here, but this scenario reeks with half-star potential.

DIANE: Let me fill you in with the facts. Falling in love and starting a family was not in my life's game plan. I was already financially independent, quite satisfied with the single life, it was an unplanned pregnancy, and I didn't seduce your husband.

ONEIDA: You think I'm unaware of the goings-on at computer networking seminars?

   Fingers accidently touching by the IBM pamphlets.

   A wayward glance during the facilitator's opening remarks.

A piece of paper wafts out of her briefcase. It lands by Robert's feet. Oh, Robert—always the gentleman.

Diane coyly peeks over Robert's shoulder as he tests a display software sample ... her cheek reflects a soft blue glow to the left of his eye ... see how he knows exactly which buttons to push ... as he catches wind of her delicately fragranced sensitive skin deodorant ... You do have sensitive skin, don't you, Diane? Of course you do. All home-wreckers have sensitive skin.

(Pause.)

Didn't you know? Diane? Didn't you know how desperately we were trying to make a baby? Truth now.

DIANE: Yes.

ONEIDA: You are a woman. You can imagine how it feels. You owe me this much. If I were to feel your baby ... I would have absolute proof. As much as it would cause me pain, it would also release me.

Please. Give me the opportunity to move on with my life.

(DIANE removes her hands from her belly and moves slightly towards ONEIDA, offering. The tension in ONEIDA's hand should at first be disturbing—perhaps she will do something harmful. DIANE tries to stop ONEIDA's hands now, but then places them herself on her abdomen. The emotion is overwhelming. After an uncomfortably long feel, ONEIDA backs up with her hands still in a cupped position. She then places them over her own stomach and exits.)

Scene Six

(The bedroom. SISTER wheels in a trolley on which there is an assortment of "surgical" supplies. Necessary are scissors, a large needle, a roll of thin, flexible beading wire, rubbing alcohol, a large can of "light" beer and a bottle of prescription pills. Also on the trolley, is the Virtual Pregnancy Monitor [VPM] and the completed cyberwomb—now a well-shaped prosthesis of an extended womb in a six-month pregnancy size, in which there is a connector hole to insert the cable from the headpiece. There are small holes around the outside edge for the "sewing," and metal straps which go up between the breasts and over the shoulders for support.

Slide images as spoken of in SISTER's speech are displayed on the set. She addresses the audience.)

SISTER: The ritualistic introduction of solid foreign substances into the flesh has been widely practised all over the world for centuries. Whether it be the intra-epidermal insertion of pebbles to create permanent lumps in a festive motif upon the face, torso or penis for ceremonial reasons ... The use of wood and bone to stretch and distort the pliable skin of the lips and earlobes into gaudy proportions for reasons of allure ... The piercing with precious metals in imaginative areas of the body for self-decoration ... Or the introduction of human-made substitutes to render functional a defunct organ ... humans have, throughout history, attempted to artificially improve upon the physical self.

(ONEIDA enters, wearing a robe, and kneels on the bed readying herself, stroking her belly. There is a ritualistic air about her actions.

SISTER pulls a length of the wire and cuts it. She then threads the wire onto the needle.)

Almost entirely without exception, every culture has found the human body to be fundamentally at a loss in some way which demands further refinement or modification by humankind.

In some instances, these procedures are regarded by the clan as spiritually necessary; rites of passage, or appeasement to the god or gods.

In others, the individual will impose this alteration upon themselves as a method of self-glorification or self-condemnation; in hopes of either redemption or damnation.

ONEIDA: Redemption ... damnation. Nonsense! I told you ... this is about protection.

(SISTER uses the alcohol and a cloth and rubs down the metal wire.)

SISTER: Occasionally, these practices can lead to poisoning, uncontrolled bleeding, internal infection and eventual death. However, with the use of carefully sterilized instruments and stringent post-operative care, it is not unfeasible to permanently adhere an alien object to the human form.

(SISTER opens the bottle of pills and hands a handful to ONEIDA.)

Commonly, before undergoing these procedures, the recipient will be administered certain incapacitators to eliminate undue pain and fear.

(SISTER then opens the can of beer and hands it to ONEIDA. ONEIDA takes a long swig.)

ONEIDA removes the robe. SISTER takes the cyberwomb from the trolley and fits it onto ONEIDA. She then hands her the needle and wire.

ONEIDA holds the needle up. Pause.)

ONEIDA: There were some things I was good for.

(ONEIDA slowly stitches the womb to herself. She works hard to overcome the pain. SISTER dabs up the blood as ONEIDA stitches.)

SISTER: At nine years old—Mom and Dad had a Christmas party.

ONEIDA: I greeted the guests at the door, and took their fur coats to my room and put them on my bed.

SISTER: Father enjoyed his martini after work.

ONEIDA: Chill the glass. Gin. Vermouth—

ONEIDA: Shake with ice.

SISTER: Two olives.

ONEIDA: Onions on Friday.

SISTER: Your academic achievements were a good reflection on them.

ONEIDA: Everyone admires the mother of a high achiever.

SISTER: But, ultimately, you were a pain in the ass.

ONEIDA: Travel arrangements were always a hassle.

SISTER: Your juvenile opinions were annoying.

ONEIDA: Fine restaurants don't have kiddy menus.

SISTER: But, most disappointingly, you were absolutely unathletically inclined.

ONEIDA: A complete klutz.

SISTER: No grace.

ONEIDA: And now this.

SISTER: You're even more unwanted now than you were before.

ONEIDA: I think you're right.

SISTER: But a baby—

ONEIDA: A baby—

SISTER: A baby *needs* its mother.

ONEIDA: A baby wants its mother.

SISTER: They know nothing else.

ONEIDA: That's their job.

(SISTER snips the wire short. She helps ONEIDA put on the VPM and makes the connections into the womb. The headpiece is now miked, supplying an echoey quality.)

Testing, testing ... one two three, one two three. Hello. Hello. *(She smiles.)* Hello ...

(ONEIDA carefully slips her robe back on, and lays down in a fetal position. SISTER wheels off the trolley. A passage of time.

The effects of shock begin to overcome ONEIDA—uncontrolled shaking and uneven breathing.

A phone rings. The answering machine clicks on.)

MACHINE: Hi. You've reached Robert and Oneida's house. You know the drill ...

(Beep.

MAUREEN appears in sailing clothes with a suitcase.

SISTER comes and helps ONEIDA put on her coat and leads her out the door. ONEIDA's following lines are voiceovers.)

ONEIDA: Sixteen weeks.

MAUREEN: Oneida, it's your mother, dear.

ONEIDA: Limbs properly formed, all joints are moving.

MAUREEN: You know I don't like talking to machines, so I'll make it quick.

ONEIDA: Vigorous movements are rarely felt by the mother. Finger- and toenails are present.

MAUREEN: I called your office, they said you haven't been in for days.

ONEIDA: Primary sex characteristics are now distinguishable. Head still disproportionately large compared to the rest of the body.

MAUREEN: I hope you haven't started moping around again.

ONEIDA: Downy hair called lanugo forms over whole fetus including the face. Growth of eyebrows and eyelashes.

MAUREEN: Life is going to pass you by, if you don't pull yourself together.

ONEIDA: Approximate length: sixteen centimetres.

MAUREEN: I called to let you know I'm going sailing with Virginia.

ONEIDA: Weight: one hundred thirty-five grams.

MAUREEN: We haven't quite decided where. We're just going to let the wind blow us where it may.

ONEIDA: Times two.

MAUREEN: I should be back in September. I'll try to keep you posted.

ONEIDA: Bon voyage.

(SISTER and ONEIDA exit.)

Scene Seven

(The reception area of a doctor's office. A pregnant RECEPTIONIST is at her desk. She wears a cyber telephone headset. ONEIDA walks in, obviously in pain, protecting her middle. It takes great strength to get through this scene.)

RECEPTIONIST: *(Into headset.)* Doctor's office ... one moment please ... *(To ONEIDA.)* Hello.

ONEIDA: I'd like to see Dr. Krumm, please.

RECEPTIONIST: I'm sorry, that's not possible.

ONEIDA: I was supposed to make an appointment, but I forgot.

RECEPTIONIST: I'm sorry, I thought we sent notices to all of his patients ... your name, please ...?

ONEIDA: I'm a special patient of his ... I'm probably not in your "regular" files.

RECEPTIONIST: I'm sorry, I'm not aware of any other files—

ONEIDA: Are you new here?

RECEPTIONIST: Just about six weeks, yes.

ONEIDA: Oh, I see ... well, could you just tell him that Oneida Kilborn is waiting, I'm sure he'll make room for me.

RECEPTIONIST: I'm sorry, Mrs. Kilborn—

ONEIDA: It's *Ms.* Kilborn.

RECEPTIONIST: I'm sorry, Ms. Kilborn—

ONEIDA: Did your parents divorce when you were very young?

RECEPTIONIST: Yes, actually.

ONEIDA: Well, you shouldn't feel guilty about that, it's not your fault. So, stop saying your sorry, nobody gives a damn! Now, how long before I can see Dr. Krumm?

RECEPTIONIST: Ms. Kilborn ... Dr. Krumm is deceased.

    (Pause.)

ONEIDA: What?

RECEPTIONIST: He died ... two weeks ago in a tragic car accident. It was very unfortunate.

ONEIDA: Oh, my god, they found out.

RECEPTIONIST: I'm sorry? I mean, pardon me?

ONEIDA: A car accident? It's like something out of a spy novel. Couldn't they have done something less dangerous to others—

RECEPTIONIST: Who?

ONEIDA: Like poison ... or a gunshot ... This is terrible!

RECEPTIONIST: Do you wish to see another doctor? You are looking for an obstetrician ...?

ONEIDA: No! Um ... No ... I have to think for a bit.

RECEPTIONIST: Are you sure you're all right? Maybe you shouldn't be walking around, if you're having a problem.

ONEIDA: No, no ... I'll take care of it.

(ONEIDA turns to leave, the RECEPTIONIST goes after her.)

RECEPTIONIST: Ms. Kilborn ... wait ... you don't look well ... perhaps you should—

ONEIDA: Get away from me!

RECEPTIONIST: Please, I just want to help you.

ONEIDA: You want to help me? Give me the name of a good antibiotic.

RECEPTIONIST: What is it for?

ONEIDA: Stop prying, lady! It could get you in trouble, too.

RECEPTIONIST: If you would just see Doctor Mehta ... she could prescribe ...

ONEIDA: I *know* what the problem is! I need an antibiotic to fight the infection!

RECEPTIONIST: Internal or external!

ONEIDA: Both!

RECEPTIONIST: Well ... polysporin for external and for internal ... you need a prescription!

ONEIDA: Just give me the name of a good one!

RECEPTIONIST: Uh ... Amoxycillin ...!

ONEIDA: How do you spell it?

RECEPTIONIST: Uh ... A–M–O—

(ONEIDA grabs a prescription pad from the desk and hands it to the RECEPTIONIST.)

ONEIDA: Write it down!

(The RECEPTIONIST writes it down. ONEIDA rips it off the pad and exits.)

Thank you.

RECEPTIONIST: But—

ONEIDA: You could lose your job for writing a prescription, could you not?

RECEPTIONIST: Maybe?

ONEIDA: So, I wouldn't tell anyone if I were you.

   (ONEIDA exits.)

RECEPTIONIST: Take it on a full stomach! *(Into headset as she exits.)* Sorry to keep you waiting ... are you experiencing any uteral discomfort ...?

   (Visual: fully formed twin fetuses.)

Scene Eight

   (The bedroom. ONEIDA is laughing deliriously. She crawls on to the bed, her head in SISTER's lap.)

ONEIDA: So, the pharmacist says: "there's no dosage indicated here, I'll have to call your physician." And I say, "Well, that might be difficult, do you have a direct line to heaven?"

Ow, don't make me laugh.

   (SISTER opens a bottle of pills and helps ONEIDA take them.)

Is the door locked?

SISTER: Yes. Let's review the facts.

ONEIDA: Krumm is dead. Robert's engaged. Mother's around Cape Horn.

SISTER: Father.

ONEIDA: Not so much as a call at Christmas.

SISTER: No connections at all.

ONEIDA: I'm operating solo.

SISTER: Needs.

ONEIDA: Two Liveability Licences.

SISTER: But if they're perfect, they should allow them.

ONEIDA: They're not going to let me get away with it. They have to set an example. They'll have to make me suffer. They are going to pull them out and send them shivering off to the Reserves!

SISTER: You can't let that happen.

ONEIDA: They are watching my every move.

SISTER: Then, why haven't they got you yet?

ONEIDA: They're waiting. It's just a matter of time.

ONEIDA: Is the door locked?

SISTER: Yes.

(ONEIDA takes several more pills.)

ONEIDA: Hook me up.

(With difficulty, SISTER helps ONEIDA up and on with the VPM, then plugs it into the womb.)

May I have a word alone?

(SISTER exits. ONEIDA steps carefully downstage centre. This speech is miked as before.)

Hello. This is your mother speaking.

I've been thinking about the day when you will go off to school. I've been thinking we'll be standing on the side of the road, waiting for the bus to come. I think it will be a foggy fall day. The sun will be trying to shine through, everything will be bathed in a golden cloud.

I will be holding one of each of your little hands, and in your other hand, clutched tight, will be a new shiny lunch box, packed with peanut butter sandwiches, carrot sticks and a cookie.

You won't know it, but in my hands I am feeling the details of yours. I am so close to your hands, that I can feel your folds and fingerprints. I am so close, I can feel the blood circulating in your palms.

You won't know it, but I am thinking about five years of your lives. Of our lives. I will be wondering if in those five years, I gave you everything you needed. Everything you needed, so that you can climb onto that bus, take your seat and drive away from me.

The bus will come too soon. The door will swing open, and I'll have no choice, no choice but to let go of your hands.

I feel naked. I feel unbalanced.

I watch you stretch your legs so high to make that big first step. I watch the door close, and then your faces appear against the window. Nervous smiles. Excitement. Fear. You're waving now, as the bus pulls away, as it disappears into the fog. You won't know it, but I am standing in the fog for a long time.

I can't see anything clearly today.

(Pause.)

This is about sacrifice. This is about protection.

(SISTER appears upstage in full cyber costume.)

SISTER: An often-told account of afterlife phenomenon places the recently deceased in a misty tunnel, at the end of which shines an extremely bright light and in which the recently deceased experiences absolute contentment and freedom.

(Slowly, ONEIDA kneels. She removes the headpiece and the womb, and places them down on the stage.)

Emerging in the tunnel to greet the recently deceased are the embodiments of those who were loved ones. These loved ones guide them towards the light with which it is assumed they become one. An assumption only, for no one who claims to have experienced such an event ever successfully proceeds beyond the end of the tunnel and returns to tell of it.

Critics of these accounts have argued that this afterlife phenomenon is merely a subconscious function of the brain, still feeding from the small amount of oxygenated blood available, and that popular culture, atop individual desire, has pre-programmed this reverie.

(ONEIDA stands and turns towards SISTER. She slowly walks back to her.)

If then, the desire of the recently deceased to experience this phenomenon can affect her final consciousness, is it out of the question to assume that she can include in the event loved ones whose existence she believed in at the time of her death?

(Children's voices are heard over. ONEIDA and SISTER speak on stage.)

MICHAEL: Mommy?

(ONEIDA looks down to her right.)

ONEIDA: Yes, Michael.

MICHAEL: If they had changed my DNA, would I have been a different person?

ONEIDA: Good question.

CHRISSY: Mommy?

(ONEIDA looks down to her left.)

ONEIDA: Yes, Chrissy?

CHRISSY: If they had made me a better person, would I have had a better soul?

ONEIDA: I don't think so.

MICHAEL: Mom?

ONEIDA: Yes?

MICHAEL: Do worms have faces?

ONEIDA: *(Chuckling.)* You know, I believe they do. Hold my hands now. I think it's time to go.

MICHAEL and CHRISSY: *(Together.)* Okay.

ONEIDA: *(To SISTER.)* Well, are you coming?

SISTER: Me?

ONEIDA: Yeah, you.

SISTER: Yeah, okay. I'm coming.

(Light slowly fades on SISTER.)

ONEIDA: This is your aunt.

MICHAEL: Hi.

CHRISSY: Hi.

SISTER: Hi.

CHRISSY: Mommy?

ONEIDA: Mm-hm?

CHRISSY: Are you happy?

ONEIDA: Oh, yes. I am the happiest Mommy in the whole ... wide ... universe.

(Lights fade on ONEIDA.

The end.)

The Slow Eviction
of Ruby Rosenholtz

by
Toby Rodin

The Slow Eviction of Ruby Rosenholtz was first read at the Tarragon Theater December 7, 1994, with the following cast:

DARLENE SAUNDERS	Clare Coulter
RUBY ROSENHOLTZ	Debra Kirshenbaum
TEDDY MEADOWS	Peter MacNeil
HOTEL MAN	Alan Williams

The play was presented at The Gathering festival in September of 1996, at the Tarragon Extra Space. It was directed by Dean Gilmour, with the following cast.

DARLENE SAUNDERS	Jackie Burroughs
RUBY ROSENHOLTZ	Debra Kirshenbaum
TEDDY MEADOWS	Duncan Ollerenshaw
HOTEL MAN	Greg Kramer

for my sister Cassie

Characters

DARLENE
RUBY
TEDDY
HOTEL MAN

Setting

The action takes place in a dilapidated hotel located in the downtown core.
The hotel functions as a rooming house for drifters and displaced persons.
The city is Vancouver, Canada. It is summertime, 1993.

Scene One

(Darlene's room, early afternoon.)

RUBY: Don't worry about me Darlene—it's nice to know someone cares, but believe me when I say this, nobody has played a head game with me and won yet. This is a minor set back in operations. I've got a plan.

DARLENE: I hope so but it's kinda hard to plan for something like that. I mean, how do you know what somebody is thinking half the time?

RUBY: Believe me I've got those bastards pegged. What I can't stand, you know what I hate? Is when people—why is it? Can you tell me why people, the second they have even the most minimal amount of authority, start behaving like laboratory rats? Why is that?

DARLENE: I don't know.

RUBY: What the hell kind of crackpot accusation is that? He actually asked me, I mean can you believe it? Who thinks this stuff up? Who?

DARLENE: You gotta remember who you're dealing with here.

RUBY: But that's just it, he won't say who saw me. Just someone.

DARLENE: Don't worry, let it ride, it'll pass. It's this place. People making stuff up in their head, pretty soon they believe it.

RUBY: I don't want any information, anything that can be held against me—a bold-faced lie on paper. Paper has been the death of millions. He has a list down there, did you know that?

DARLENE: Yeah, but he writes everything in pencil, it's not a real list.

RUBY: Have you seen it? How do you know? Darlene, you've got to tell me what it looks like. Tell me—tell me exactly what it looks like.

DARLENE: It's nothing. It's a pink Hilroy scribbler with some phone numbers for Chinese food taped on the cover.

RUBY: It's not nothing, I'm in it! He told me, "You're on the list Ruby." I've got to see the list, it's crucial. Boy I can't wait to find out who "somebody" is. I'll murder them alive when I do.

DARLENE: Then you'll be on a list for sure.

RUBY: Someone has got it in for me. Spreading lies and writing them in a pink scribbler. You just proved it.

DARLENE: I guarantee you nobody has written a word.

RUBY: It's a mark, a strike against me. You've got to believe me, Darlene. We have to get me erased from this list.

DARLENE: We'll get you off it, now calm yourself down for a minute.

RUBY: Because the last thing I need in my life right now is more stress and persecution.

DARLENE: No, no one needs that.

RUBY: Damn, everything was going perfectly, and now this.

DARLENE: What does he want, did he say?

RUBY: Oh God, no.

DARLENE: You know what I think happened? I think maybe you scared one of the guys upstairs or something.

RUBY: "Scared"? What do you mean "scared"? I'm not scaring anyone, they're scaring me.

DARLENE: There's no women around this place you gotta remember that. Some of those boys are pretty jumpy.

RUBY: For Christ, Darlene, I don't walk up and down the corridors trying to sex people up, I don't even have sex. In fact, people accuse me of behaving like a man. Did you know that?

DARLENE: Yeah, I know that. What did he say?

RUBY: It was basically an accusation. He said, "Ruby, have you been walking around the hotel naked? Have you been knocking on people's doors in the middle of the night without any clothes on?"

DARLENE: That was this morning?

RUBY: First thing. I came back from Shoppers Drug Mart with my prescription, which is almost gone now because I didn't want to get depressed. I took too much but it's not working because by tomorrow or the day after I won't have any left at all and that is depressing me even more than this goddamned list.

DARLENE: Why don't we have some cheese toast and watch Oprah. Last week a woman came on and was saying how her father was having sexual intercourse with her and her brother since they were two. And her worst memory was he locked her in a well full of snakes. Poor lady got one hundred and twenty-seven personalities.

RUBY: Oh Christ that's disgusting. It goes to show you some people should not have children.

DARLENE: It was really sad, Oprah was in tears. She has a daughter, her daughter came on TV with her. Only thing they can't do is go to pet stores together on account of the snakes.

RUBY: Snakes eh? My father never pulled any of that touchy-feely stuff. My childhood was blessed, I never had sex with my parents, not once.

DARLENE: We can't have any cheese toast, there's no bread. I'm starving.

RUBY: Do you want to hear my plan?

DARLENE: Sure, okay.

RUBY: There's safety in numbers, my father told me that. My plan is basically this: when I go down to get myself off the list you come with me. We go down together.

DARLENE: Together, eh? You want me to phone Jerry, he could swing by—

RUBY: No not Jerry! Promise me you won't breathe a word of this to Jerry. It's strictly between us. You and me together.

DARLENE: Why together?

RUBY: He likes you way better.

DARLENE: No he doesn't.

RUBY: Of course he does.

DARLENE: How do you know what he likes?

RUBY: Don't play dumb, Darlene. You're his favorite.

DARLENE: What makes you say that?

RUBY: He's pegged me as a hothead and you're the big wise saint.

DARLENE: Oh boy, saint. I don't know about that.

RUBY: You have to do the talking. He can't stand the sight of me.

DARLENE: What am I supposed to say?

RUBY: Tell him I'm your friend, I'm your best friend. It's crucial he knows people care about me.

DARLENE: You gotta learn to keep your mouth shut, I mean it.

RUBY: You're absolutely right, my temper is the shits.

DARLENE: Everything will be fine so long as you don't fly off the handle when we explain it.

RUBY: I just had a brainstorm. You go talk to him and I'll wait up here. I don't want to screw it up.

DARLENE: You want me to go alone?

RUBY: The last thing we want is to start a bloodbath at the front desk. We don't want a war on our hands, just to get the point across simply. He'll listen to you a hell of a lot better if I'm not around.

DARLENE: What am I supposed to say?

RUBY: Anything, I want him to see I have friends. It's crucial he knows people care about me. I want him to know that.

DARLENE: You have me and you have Ted, two friends. You're doing fine. You just have to calm down, 'cause I'll tell you something about the rolling stone who gathered no moss, she cracked her head open. And that's the truth.

Scene Two

(Early morning, the following day. HOTEL MAN is behind the front desk of the hotel lobby when DARLENE enters.)

DARLENE: It's dark in here, my eyes are all screwed up. It sure is bright out there.

HOTEL MAN: Isn't the day spectacular?

DARLENE: Yes, it certainly is hot out there and very blue, the sky.

HOTEL MAN: Wonderful. Is there a breeze, I love a breeze?

DARLENE: No, no breeze.

HOTEL MAN: Too bad. You're up early, it's good. Take advantage of the light while it lasts.

DARLENE: Yes it's summer now, isn't it?

HOTEL MAN: Oh yes, it's summer.

DARLENE: Not spring.

HOTEL MAN: No, it's definitely summer.

DARLENE: Good, I'm glad, I like summer.

HOTEL MAN: Of course you do.

DARLENE: Is there any mail?

HOTEL MAN: Were you expecting mail?

DARLENE: No.

HOTEL MAN: I see. Let me check for you.

DARLENE: Thank you.

HOTEL MAN: No, no mail. Flyers, a lot of flyers, and a sample of shampoo. This has got to be the bluest shampoo I've ever seen in my life, it's so blue. Would you like it? Here take it, I want you to have it. Go on take it, it's only a sample.

DARLENE: Oh thanks, that's nice. Thank you.

HOTEL MAN: You don't have to worry about anything. I believe in you, you're not like the rest.

DARLENE: I'm not like who?

HOTEL MAN: The others.

DARLENE: Which others?

HOTEL MAN: I don't wish to be indiscreet, I'm the height of discretion. But you're not like them.

DARLENE: Is everything all right?

HOTEL MAN: For you, of course, my dear.

DARLENE: People are sorta talking. I was wondering—

HOTEL MAN: Talking, what about?

DARLENE: Complaints, are people complaining about each other?

HOTEL MAN: Probably.

DARLENE: No, I mean—

HOTEL MAN: Sorry?

DARLENE: Is there—is something going on?

HOTEL MAN: Nothing that involves you, no.

DARLENE: Who does it involve?

HOTEL MAN: That I can't say.

DARLENE: Because my friend—

HOTEL MAN: Your friend who?

DARLENE: Ruby.

HOTEL MAN: Oh, Ruby.

DARLENE: It isn't true what they said, you know. She keeps to herself. I know her and the last thing on her mind is—

HOTEL MAN: Is?

DARLENE: Ruby might be a lot of things but she's not—

HOTEL MAN: It doesn't matter, it was only a warning.

DARLENE: A lot of stuff doesn't even occur to her, doesn't even cross her mind.

HOTEL MAN: Yes, it's true. She's lucky to have a friend like you.

DARLENE: Is she in any kind of trouble?

HOTEL MAN: Not trouble, no, I wouldn't call it that.

DARLENE: I know there's a note pad around here somewhere. I was wondering if maybe I could have a look at it.

HOTEL MAN: The scribbler. I can show it to you.

DARLENE: I'd like to have a look at it.

(*HOTEL MAN retrieves a pink Hilroy scribbler from behind the desk.*)

HOTEL MAN: By all means. You can see for yourself it's quite flimsy.

DARLENE: Can I open it, do you mind?

HOTEL MAN: No, I don't really. Just keep it under your hat will you, that's all I ask.

DARLENE: Is it some kind of secret or something?

HOTEL MAN: No, but there's no real reason for you to see it. You're not in it.

DARLENE: Ruby is.

HOTEL MAN: Yes she is. Twice in fact.

DARLENE: Two times, are you sure?

HOTEL MAN: Look for yourself.

DARLENE: I don't think she even knows about the second one.

HOTEL MAN: You mean the first one. No, it's likely she doesn't. I don't say anything the first time. It's always best to wait.

DARLENE: How can she get her name out of this thing?

HOTEL MAN: She can't, it goes onto her record.

DARLENE: What does all this mean?

HOTEL MAN: To be honest, nothing—not yet anyway.

DARLENE: I don't want anything to happen to her.

HOTEL MAN: Neither do I, believe me. Her life is hard and somehow she manages to make it harder. It's always the way.

DARLENE: Can you scratch out the first one ... here, March seventh "Ruby screaming, foul language banging doors and walls." I know it's asking a lot, but if you let me talk to her she'll stop ... it's not always easy to get through but she'll listen to me.

HOTEL MAN: You're a lovely woman, you are. I'll help you this once but it doesn't matter with her kind. It's only a matter of time before she trips herself again.

DARLENE: Thank you, thank you so much.

(*DARLENE goes to exit and turns quickly.*)

And thank you for the shampoo too.

Scene Three

(Darlene's room, later the same day. DARLENE is in the bathroom with the door locked. RUBY is standing outside the door, knocking.)

RUBY: Darlene? Darlene, are you in the bathroom? It's okay if you're in the bathroom, stay in the bathroom. I just have to get something off my chest. I don't want to disrupt your day but I tell ya I'm going to strangle the fucking pharmacist, him and his assistant. He looks like Bela Lugosi and she looks like a Pekinese. I hate people who stare and whisper deliberately—loud enough for you to hear, "She took six pills at once." I wanted to scream, "Yes, the second I'm out the door and around the corner I'll take six more. I'm a drug addict, everyone." What a joke, I would love to be a drug addict—the hard cold facts are I can't afford to be a drug addict. I could knock back my monthly prescription in about three minutes. So, yes, I guess you could say my tolerance is a little high, but the two of them, they treat me like I've come crawling out of a gutter with yellow crust on my eye begging for a fix. Well I've got news for them, it's not a fix, it's a prescription—

(DARLENE opens the bathroom door. She is holding the sample of shampoo.)

DARLENE: You don't listen to a word I say. Why do I bother sometimes, why do I even bother.

RUBY: No I remember, I remember every word you said. Roll with the punches—I remember, see? Roll with the punches, and I am, Darlene, it's exactly what I'm doing, rolling along beautifully.

DARLENE: They don't care about you. I am always amazed by the energy you can invest in people who wouldn't notice if you dropped off the face of the earth.

RUBY: I'm not investing in Bela Lugosi and the Pekinese believe me. I'm whizzed up that's all, but basically I'm fine really. I've got my Prozac and I've got my bus pass, life couldn't be going more smoothly.

DARLENE: Did you see the hole in the wall?

RUBY: I didn't see any hole, no. Where?

DARLENE: In the lobby. I can't believe you didn't see it.

RUBY: What do you mean?

DARLENE: Our phone is gone. They ripped the phone out of the wall.

RUBY: Who ripped it out, who?

DARLENE: I don't know.

RUBY: Oh boy.

DARLENE: The hole is an omen. As soon as I saw the hole I knew it was trying to tell me something. The hole is not accidental, oh no ... the hole is serious. Yesterday we had a phone, today we have a hole. You can't take something like that lightly.

RUBY: I didn't even see it.

DARLENE: I'm going to get a job.

RUBY: What, why would you want to do that? Because of the hole?

DARLENE: Yes.

RUBY: Really, maybe I should go look at it.

DARLENE: Not only because of the hole. Partly because of Margaret, partly because of me, but the hole was the deciding factor.

RUBY: Who's Margaret?

DARLENE: The woman at the health centre, the one who wears the green sweater.

RUBY: The redhead?

DARLENE: Yes, she's Margaret.

RUBY: Margaret, that's a name you can trust.

DARLENE: Her niece died of cancer last week. The woman goes in to get iron supplements 'cause she's tired all the time and there's these little tiny bruises popping up all over her body. The doctors run some tests and three hours later she's rushed to emergency. Turns out she's riddled with cancer. They diagnosed her on the Monday afternoon put her in surgery Tuesday by late Sunday night she was gone. Poor Margaret. She looks me right in the eye and says, "No warning whatsoever. My niece was dead in eight days. Enjoy your lunch, dear, spend your money."

RUBY: Dead in eight days, boy it really isn't much warning. But on the bright side, now you know her name is Margaret.

DARLENE: Margaret pulled all the recipe cards off the bulletin boards and pushed them in my pocket. She said these are for you take them. I want you to have them. The cards didn't seem important to me until I saw the hole.

RUBY: Hey, if you got a job you could buy us lipsticks!

DARLENE: Are you listening? This is important.

RUBY: Of course sure, sure I'm listening.

DARLENE: That phone was the one thing, the only thing, in this crummy hotel that was there for us. It was ours. Mark my words the phone is only the beginning.

RUBY: I hope you're wrong.

DARLENE: Well, I hope so too, but I'm not.

RUBY: We deserve a little lipstick. Let's face the facts, we need lipstick.

DARLENE: Don't go spending all my money on lipstick, I haven't even filled out an application form.

RUBY: Boy you have guts. I wouldn't touch the work force again with a barge pole.

DARLENE: I want some pocket money, I'm a grown woman.

RUBY: I used to fantasize about being a cashier. Cashiers are classy.

DARLENE: Jerry won't be able to call me anymore. Just as well there's nothing between us, hasn't been for months. He just likes to keep me hanging.

RUBY: I saw Jerry walking down Hornby street with the midget prostitute.

DARLENE: So.

RUBY: What if he's screwing the midget prostitute?

DARLENE: Jerry wouldn't sleep with the midget, she wears burgundy eye shadow. I don't care anymore.

RUBY: Jerry's a selfish pig, and anyway, he stabs people. You don't want a boyfriend like that.

DARLENE: Margaret's going to do all my photocopying and she's going to write me a cover letter. I'm going to get a job, I can feel it in the air.

RUBY: Boy, if you got a job it would be great. It would drive Jerry nuts.

DARLENE: If you don't have a good cover letter you won't get the job. Margaret knows all the tricks.

RUBY: Just make sure you don't work for assholes. Some of these employer types are so insensitive it can tear your heart out.

DARLENE: You've got to take some risks.

RUBY: I take risks, I take lots of risks. My doctor told me I'm not cut out for the work force and I believe him. You don't have to work to be a good person.

DARLENE: I have to stop talking to the walls, it's not good for my confidence. I keep buying kaiser buns and they keep going stale before I have a chance to eat them. It's not fun.

RUBY: It could be a lot worse.

DARLENE: Stop saying that. I don't want it to be worse, I want it to be better.

RUBY: I'd be the happiest person in the world if things got better.

DARLENE: I don't have anything.

RUBY: You have a drug plan, I bet Jerry doesn't have a drug plan.

DARLENE: He doesn't need one.

RUBY: See what I mean.

DARLENE: No, I don't. I can do better than this.

RUBY: We're not on the street, Jerry's on the street. He lives in his car, for Christ's sake.

DARLENE: Shut up about Jerry. I need something to look forward to.

RUBY: I think a job is a wonderful idea.

DARLENE: He makes me sick. I mean, you'd think he'd have a bit more pride than that. He's really showing his hand. Did he see you?

RUBY: Who?

DARLENE: Jerry, when he was with the midget, did he see you see him?

RUBY: I don't know.

DARLENE: He must think he's invisible or he thinks the city's larger than it is. The city's never large when you live in it. You see everyone everywhere.

RUBY: I know it's scary. I keep trying to avoid people.

DARLENE: I always find out about everything but I pretend not to know anything. I never let on differently. I never tell them I know but I do, always. I think it's incredibly stupid of them, though, don't you?

RUBY: Of course it's stupid, what do you mean?

DARLENE: I mean it's so stupid to not even be able to imagine I might know. The chance of my finding out about these sorts of things is quite high.

RUBY: You should tell a lot more people to go to hell.

DARLENE: I don't want to show my hand. I don't even want them to know I care. But I want to know what I'm up against. Jerry's a pathological liar, do you know how I know?

RUBY: Because he lies?

DARLENE: No, because he constantly accuses everybody else of being one. He's so transparent.

RUBY: I don't know how you can stand him.

DARLENE: Anybody who won't lend him money or get into bed with him is a pathological liar. Isn't that convenient?

RUBY: Stick with Margaret, she knows the way.

DARLENE: Yes, she's going to put me in touch with Atlas Industrial

Carpet Company. They send their carpets out all over the province. Not only do they manufacture carpets but they provide a cleaning service as well. They handle every aspect of the carpet industry you could imagine.

RUBY: You mean like wall to wall broadloom?

DARLENE: No not broadloom, the broadloom industry is saturated. Atlas Industrial make mats.

RUBY: Mats?

DARLENE: Yes long red mats with rubber bottoms, to prevent people from slipping. Their mats are everywhere, grocery stores, shopping malls, movie theaters. This company is sort of famous for their mats, their mats are functional.

RUBY: What do they do?

DARLENE: These mats save people's lives. They prevent people from slipping.

RUBY: Slipping, eh?

DARLENE: Yes, slipping. I wish he'd move. I can't move, I don't have anywhere to go. But he could move, he could live anywhere. Have you ever watched him smoke?

RUBY: No.

DARLENE: Every time he lights a cigarette I want to stand up and applaud.

RUBY: He won't change Darlene. Forget him.

DARLENE: I did until you brought him up.

RUBY: I didn't, you did. You brought him up with the phone.

DARLENE: Oh yes the phone. Now we have holes in the wall to match the holes in our head. I can't just sit here stewing over an imbecile who lives in a car. I've got to make some changes. I can't go on like this, not at my age, it's not right. I have to do something.

    (TEDDY enters.)

TEDDY: They just carried a body out of here, it's right outside my window. I couldn't see the head or the feet, it's in a sleeping bag, there's a towel across the face. I could see the arms. They just stuck it in the back seat of a taxi like it was groceries. It isn't too big of a body but it isn't a small one either. It must be a man, you wouldn't put a woman's body in the back seat of a taxi, would you? I don't think you would, not in the middle of the afternoon. If it was a woman they wouldn't have been so casual, so I doubt it was a woman. Hardly any women live here. It was the body in the back seat and the driver in the front seat, just so.

Nobody else got in. I swear some of those taxis will take anyone anywhere. Nobody was rushing, the driver was rubbing his forehead. If you were in a rush you'd call an ambulance right? But this isn't an ambulance, this is a taxi. Two people carried this body no problem. Who is it do you think? Whoever it is has skinny arms. I have skinny arms. Men with skinny arms never wear T-shirts. It's why you never know they have skinny arms 'cause they hide them behind sleeves even in summer. Big bony elbows, big bony knees, it's how you can tell. The joints jump out at you. No muscle, no fat, it's scary, skinny people scare me. I'm skinny, I scare myself sometimes. Do you ever scare yourself?

DARLENE: Every day.

(TEDDY exits briefly.)

RUBY: Oh my God ...

(TEDDY re-enters.)

TEDDY: It's Mr. Horowitz. They took the towel off his face. He's dead, Mr. Horowitz is dead.

Scene Four

(The hotel lobby. RUBY is going through Hotel Man's desk in search of the list. HOTEL MAN sees her. He watches her before he stops her.)

HOTEL MAN: Are you looking for something?

RUBY: Oh hi, sorry. Nobody was here.

HOTEL MAN: I'm always here, what are you doing?

RUBY: Me? Nothing.

HOTEL MAN: The information in these drawers belongs to me. It is strictly confidential.

RUBY: Oh god, really?

HOTEL MAN: Yes, really.

RUBY: I had no idea. My father is sending me birthday money and I thought maybe it was in—it's not my birthday today or anything but I was just checking. Just trying to—

HOTEL MAN: I'm well aware of what you were trying to do. Don't try it again.

RUBY: I just wanted to see if everything is fair. Fairness counts for everything.

HOTEL MAN: I'm accurate, if that's what you mean.

RUBY: Accurate, great, even better. Some people listen to vicious lies and rumors they're so bored they'll believe anything. But you're not like that you're accurate.

HOTEL MAN: People talk at me incessantly, it's hard to know what to believe.

RUBY: I bet it is. What a tough job. I'm glad somebody's keeping a sharp eye. I have a lot of admiration for people like you.

HOTEL MAN: You're a provocateur.

RUBY: What's that supposed to mean?

HOTEL MAN: You lack restraint.

RUBY: I don't it's them. I'm trying to tell you—

HOTEL MAN: You can't control everyone and everything around you, it's not possible. If people like you they like you and if they don't, well—

RUBY: People love me!

HOTEL MAN: I'm sure they do. There's no need to get defensive.

RUBY: Sometimes I feel like I'm going to kill someone.

HOTEL MAN: Yes, I'm sure you do ... feel the way you do.

RUBY: I hate trying to explain something I haven't done. Why should I—

HOTEL MAN: No one has asked you to.

RUBY: People are ganging up on me and they're such goddamn cowards they won't even face me.

HOTEL MAN: Your behavior is aggressive and confrontational and for those reasons people may not want to.

RUBY: So what? The two old drunks upstairs beg me to give them hand jobs about five times a day. I don't report them.

HOTEL MAN: Why not?

RUBY: Because I'm not a goddamned back-stabber.

HOTEL MAN: If you complained they might stop.

RUBY: I don't really give a shit what they do.

HOTEL MAN: You should.

RUBY: They're not hurting anyone.

HOTEL MAN: I wouldn't know.

RUBY: Darlene knows I'm innocent. You believe Darlene, don't you?

HOTEL MAN: Yes, I do.

RUBY: Well, Darlene is my best friend—I'm her best friend. If that isn't proof I don't know what is.

HOTEL MAN: Darlene isn't thinking of leaving, is she?

RUBY: Oh no, she's just a bit worried about money. We all worry, but she worries more.

HOTEL MAN: She doesn't look worried, she looks determined.

RUBY: Darlene's just trying to get a bit more ambitious about making things happen.

HOTEL MAN: Where does she go every morning?

RUBY: The health centre, to see Margaret.

HOTEL MAN: Is she taking a class?

RUBY: No, she's just trying to see what her options are, you know, scouting around and checking things out. Margaret is writing her a few little letters, giving her some phone numbers, you know, contacts.

HOTEL: She's looking for a job.

RUBY: I can't tell you, it's a secret.

HOTEL MAN: I see.

Scene Five

(The hotel lobby, three days later. It is early evening. DARLENE and HOTEL MAN are together at the front desk of the lobby.)

HOTEL MAN: All I dream about these days is getting a good hair cut.

DARLENE: A lot of men would die to have your hair. It doesn't recede.

HOTEL MAN: I know, it's odd. It's my father's hair.

DARLENE: It looks really sturdy. It's never gonna fall out, not in a million years.

HOTEL MAN: Nope, it's true. I'll always have my hair. It's luck. My father told me to count my luck, so I do. My hair, my health, my youth. It's dwindling but there. My sanity, sort of on par with my youth.

DARLENE: Your job.

HOTEL MAN: The job isn't luck, it's un-luck. It's unpaid, it's unlit, it's ... I don't even know what it is anymore.

DARLENE: It could be worse, much worse.

HOTEL MAN: Don't say that to me. When I think about all the possibilities of "much worse" I nearly collapse.

DARLENE: Oh, sorry.

HOTEL MAN: I can't bear to think about it.

DARLENE: So don't.

HOTEL MAN: I've got to get out.

DARLENE: Why?

HOTEL MAN: It's getting to me. It's getting to me, it is.

DARLENE: What is?

HOTEL MAN: Nothing.

DARLENE: Are you all right? Your face is sweating.

HOTEL MAN: Is it? I'm not surprised, they're isn't any air.

DARLENE: Is it because of what happened to Mr. Horowitz, the man on the third floor?

HOTEL MAN: He certainly didn't help.

DARLENE: I guess you haven't seen many dead people.

HOTEL MAN: No, not like that. He wasn't even dressed, he looked pregnant.

DARLENE: What did you do with all his stuff?

HOTEL MAN: I got rid of it.

DARLENE: All of it?

HOTEL MAN: He didn't have much.

DARLENE: No, he didn't. Where did they take him?

HOTEL MAN: The same place they take everyone else probably.

DARLENE: Where is that?

HOTEL MAN: I don't know.

DARLENE: Was there a service?

HOTEL MAN: Of sorts, yes, I suppose there was.

DARLENE: I wish I'd known about it sooner. I'd go, I like services.

HOTEL MAN: You knew him fairly well then?

DARLENE: No, but he lived here. We should've been on the ball and given him a proper service, don't you think?

HOTEL MAN: I need someone who really knows how to cut hair. Always ask first, "Do you cut or style hair?" Avoid stylists like the plague. Cutting is an art, style is garbage.

DARLENE: I cut my own hair.

HOTEL MAN: Really? Good for you, I love it when people take risks like that. I think it's great.

DARLENE: He died on Friday?

HOTEL MAN: No, Thursday morning.

DARLENE: Couldn't have been Thursday. We saw him in line collecting his cheque.

HOTEL MAN: Perhaps it was Friday then, I can't remember. There's not really much one can do, there isn't. But I'm glad you're thinking of him, I am.

DARLENE: He's not the first to go.

HOTEL MAN: He won't be the last either. Your friend Teddy isn't lagging far behind. I worry about that one, I do.

DARLENE: Don't worry about Ted, he's tough. Ted can take it, he'll outlive us all. You'll go bald before we lose Ted.

HOTEL MAN: My father never went bald.

DARLENE: Teddy's a skinny little thing but he's strong. He's sorta like dental floss.

HOTEL MAN: It's an interesting comparison. But dental floss isn't particularly strong. For that matter neither is Ted.

DARLENE: A wire then, yes, he's more like a wire. 'Cause he's not the way he looks is all I'm saying.

HOTEL MAN: It's good to hear that, it is. If he could only find a way to adjust himself a little.

DARLENE: Oh, he's getting better. Ruby takes care of him, makes him eat. Ted's not much of an eater.

HOTEL MAN: Serious drinkers never are. He's so sweet, such a sweet, sweet man. Teddy's an angel, he is. I know it.

DARLENE: Yes, I think so too.

HOTEL MAN: And you're a saint, my love.

DARLENE: Well, I hear voices but I'm no saint, believe me.

HOTEL MAN: All the great saints were completely unhinged. Did you know that?

DARLENE: I take medication now.

HOTEL MAN: Maybe you should stop, you're radiant.

DARLENE: I remember walking through Eaton's and God started brushing my hair when I was standing on the escalator.

HOTEL MAN: Maybe you shouldn't stop. I'm sorry, that was mean. Your encounter on the escalator sounds charming.

DARLENE: Nobody's ever been murdered in this hotel. The people who live here are making an effort. We are all trying to get along.

HOTEL MAN: You're absolutely right. But don't tempt fate, my love, don't.

DARLENE: I won't.

HOTEL MAN: You just did but never mind. What's happening with your friend Ruby, she's been keeping a low profile.

DARLENE: Oh she's around.

HOTEL MAN: Keeps erratic hours, doesn't she?

DARLENE: Yeah, her sleep patterns are a little different. She has problems relaxing.

HOTEL MAN: Maybe it's the noise. I can't stand the noise, I bet it's the noise.

DARLENE: Could be.

HOTEL MAN: The traffic doesn't stop. You can't make it stop, it's relentless.

DARLENE: Oh yeah, your room faces the street, doesn't it?

HOTEL MAN: All the rooms face the street.

DARLENE: Are they making you dress up for the job? I've never seen you wear a tie before.

HOTEL MAN: No, I was trying to impress you. Have I succeeded?

DARLENE: It's beautiful … it's a beautiful old tie.

HOTEL MAN: Isn't it, though, I got it at the Sally Ann for seventy-five cents. It was the bargain of the century.

DARLENE: It's almost in perfect condition.

HOTEL MAN: I know it's fabulous. It just goes to show you, you don't have to spend a lot of money to look half-way interesting.

DARLENE: No I guess not.

HOTEL MAN: Sewing from the thirties, there's nothing like it. Those clothes are still with us, it blows my mind. The depression was almost worth it for the fashion alone.

DARLENE: I'm glad you said almost.

HOTEL MAN: Darlene, you're looking so pensive.

DARLENE: I'm just thinking … what I should eat for dinner?

HOTEL MAN: I'm starving. Let's order in some Chinese, my treat.

DARLENE: No, I better go see what Ruby and Ted are up to.

HOTEL MAN: Ruby and Ted? I can guarantee you right now, nothing. C'mon stay, live on the edge.

DARLENE: I do.

(DARLENE exits.)

Scene Six

(Darlene's room, later the same evening. She and TEDDY have been talking together prior to RUBY bursting in.)

RUBY: Ha, caught ya! Talking behind my back again, don't try to deny it now, kiddies. I've got X-ray ears, heard every word, ya buggers!

TEDDY: Good, then we won't have to repeat ourselves.

RUBY: *(To DARLENE.)* Hey you, you big fat loser, gimme your kaiser bun.

DARLENE: Hey loser, lose weight loser.

RUBY: Hey loser, go take a class.

DARLENE: Go take an overdose.

RUBY: You don't have a VCR.

DARLENE: You don't have a boyfriend.

RUBY: You don't have prospects.

DARLENE: Are you a virgin?

RUBY: Are you a mental case?

DARLENE: Are you a liar?

RUBY: Are you a subscriber?

DARLENE: Are you a lesbo?

RUBY: Are you allergic?

DARLENE: Are you suicidal?

TEDDY: Hey, tell Ruby what you told me.

DARLENE: I've got a story for you about Hotel Man.

RUBY: What—what happened?

TEDDY: Hotel Man was wearing Mr. Horowitz's tie. He ripped off Horowitz's tie.

RUBY: Really? No, way. I'm glad you said that, you won't believe—

TEDDY: He thinks we're all too crazy or plastered to notice!

DARLENE: Thanks for letting me tell my story, Ted.

TEDDY: Sorry.

RUBY: Wait, fuck you guys—wait till you hear this. I saw the bastard wearing green cuff links. And I thought, man I've seen those before. It was almost like de ja vu. I said, "Wow, where'd you get those?" He shot me the dirtiest fuckin' look and said, "Ruby are you wearing a bra?" No, he didn't say "bra," he said "brassiere." "Ruby, are you wearing a brassiere by any chance?" I thought, what the hell kind of a question is that? The guy's obviously in a pissy mood, whatever. But it's coming back to me now, crystal clear. Darlene, remember, Horowitz kept green cuff links in an egg cup by his bed? He just had them sitting there by his bed.

DARLENE: Yeah I know, the egg cup. It had a wedding ring in it too.

RUBY: That's right, a little diamond and green cuff links. I'd like to push his head through a wall. He's not even trying to fuckin' well hide it.

TEDDY: When I die don't let nobody lay a hand on me or my stuff. Wrap every thing up in a big green garbage bag an'—

DARLENE: Shut up Ted.

RUBY: Every time somebody in this place kicks off he's in there like a rat clearing out their goddamn room.

DARLENE: It's not the first time, eh?

RUBY: Of course not.

TEDDY: Horowitz wanted to wear all that stuff in his casket, I bet ya. Tie, ring, cuff links. Sure makes sense, probably figured people would organize it an' make sure he looked nice 'n' classy.

DARLENE: He didn't figure on the front desk.

TEDDY: You want to look your best. I'm gonna wear my blue shirt and my grey cords, keep it simple.

DARLENE: What?

TEDDY: No makeup.

DARLENE: Ted, I told ya, shut up.

TEDDY: Fine, I'll shut up. Just don't let them make me wear false eye lashes. It's hard enough being dead.

DARLENE: One minute you want to be in a green garbage bag, the next you want to be in your grey cords. Which is it?

TEDDY: Forget it.

RUBY: And he has the nerve—the goddamn nerve to threaten me. Him and his big secret list. I might be neurotic, but I sure as hell don't steal from stiffs.

TEDDY: Footwear isn't so important.

DARLENE: *(To TEDDY.)* Would you stop daydreaming about death, we're trying to figure something out here.

TEDDY: I'm helping.

RUBY: They're all scared of my tits.

TEDDY: Breasts make people very nervous, even children.

DARLENE: *(To RUBY.)* I don't think he's figured you out yet.

RUBY: This makes my blood boil.

DARLENE: Don't start screaming, I'm trying to get you off the list.

RUBY: What else did he say? Did he say anything about me?

DARLENE: No, he didn't say anything about you this time.

RUBY: Who did he talk about?

DARLENE: Himself.

RUBY: What did he say?

DARLENE: I think he's sort of falling apart. He hates the hotel and he hates his life. So he's going to get a haircut.

RUBY: A haircut, eh? I'd give anything to be his barber for two minutes.

DARLENE: The only thing he likes about himself is his hair. I didn't have the heart to tell him, "Mister, your hair looks like it's been set on fire."

TEDDY: I'm trying to remember seeing people's feet. I can't. Do they cover up the feet? With cloth, or with flowers ... Do they cover the feet with flowers?

DARLENE: Nothing happens to the feet. Now he's worried about his feet.

TEDDY: I'm not.

RUBY: Teddy's going to live to be a hundred and ten, aren't you Ted?

TEDDY: No.

DARLENE: He can keep up his end in a conversation, I'll give him that much.

TEDDY: Don't let them bully me into cremation. They'll try, don't let them.

DARLENE: What have you got against cremation?

TEDDY: It's not for me.

DARLENE: Cremation is ancient, it's highly respected.

TEDDY: It's not for me.

DARLENE: Fine.

RUBY: We could store you in your wife's teapot—just kidding.

TEDDY: No.

DARLENE: Poor old Mr. Horowitz he didn't stand a chance. Hotel Man probably had his eye on those green cuff links for months. The tie was just a bonus.

RUBY: Who's gonna pay for your funeral Ted? Funerals aren't cheap.

TEDDY: The city, who else?

RUBY: Oh good, I thought we'd have to take up a collection. Boy, if it was left up to us you'd wind up in a blue box—just kidding.

TEDDY: Thanks a bunch.

DARLENE: I hope they give you a choice. I mean if you pay you get a choice but if the city pays does the city decide?

TEDDY: No, dummy, I decide, I'm the one who's dead. It's my big day, why do you think I'm telling you for?

DARLENE: *(To RUBY.)* We're going to have to mud wrestle with the funeral director by the sounds of it.

TEDDY: I want to be buried.

DARLENE: It doesn't sound like you've done much research.

TEDDY: I know what I want.

DARLENE: For someone who doesn't think anything through you're very set in your ways.

RUBY: I just got a horrible flash, what if Hotel Man decides?

TEDDY: Great, I can see where this is going.

RUBY: He hustled Horowitz out of here before anyone could bat an eye. Sneaky bastard.

TEDDY: Wrapped him up in a sleeping bag and stuck him in a taxi. I wonder who was driving that taxi.

DARLENE: Some of those taxi drivers are pretty bizarre.

TEDDY: That's not going to happen to me—

RUBY: Don't worry, pussycat, we'd never let it happen to you in a million years.

TEDDY: I hope not.

DARLENE: We won't.

TEDDY: He kept the towel, he took it back.

DARLENE: What?

TEDDY: They put a towel across Horowitz's face. He took it off and brought it back in the hotel.

RUBY: Are you serious?

TEDDY: He's afraid of losing a towel.

DARLENE: I still don't know where they buried him. I don't think it was anywhere central.

TEDDY: What do you mean, "central"?

DARLENE: Well nobody seems to know. I haven't heard anything.

RUBY: If you want to find out anything, you better find it out fast.

DARLENE: Yes, I think so too.

TEDDY: You mean downtown?

DARLENE: What?

TEDDY: You don't think he's still in the city?

DARLENE: No, I don't.

TEDDY: I do.

DARLENE: You do, how's that?

TEDDY: He lived here all his life.

DARLENE: They don't know that, people do as their told.

RUBY: I think he's in the lake—just kidding.

TEDDY: Where would they take him?

DARLENE: Somewhere along the outskirts, it's cheaper.

TEDDY: What's cheaper?

DARLENE: Land, plots, I don't know, everything I guess.

TEDDY: I knew a guy who worked in a crematorium he said it took a long time and there was always something left behind afterwards. And when they do it all the windows in the building shake. They shake and they shake and they shake.

Scene Seven

(The hotel lobby, late afternoon. A small celebration has been prepared for DARLENE. HOTEL MAN has organized the event. TEDDY has been put in charge of blowing up the balloons. RUBY hovers over the cake, periodically tapping it with her fingers.)

HOTEL MAN: Ruby, get your little mitts off the icing. Has everyone signed the card?

RUBY: Doesn't this frosting look like cement? Luckily looks are deceptive; it's very soft.

HOTEL MAN: Get away from the cake. Where's the card gone, Teddy?

(RUBY moves away from the cake.)

TEDDY: It was here a minute ago, I put it right ... *(TEDDY stands, he has been sitting on it.)* Here it is, uh oh, the envelope is bent.

HOTEL MAN: Give it to me.

TEDDY: I didn't sign it yet.

(He signs the card and gives it to HOTEL MAN.)

Don't make us sing "Happy Birthday," it's a terrible song.

HOTEL MAN: Ted.

TEDDY: What?

HOTEL MAN: It's not her birthday.

TEDDY: It's not.

HOTEL MAN: No.

TEDDY: What is it then?

HOTEL MAN: It's a celebration for her new job.

TEDDY: What job?

HOTEL MAN: Darlene works now, she's at work. Didn't you know?

TEDDY: No, she never said nothing to me about no job. Christ, you're all
so secretive.

HOTEL MAN: She didn't want anyone to know.

TEDDY: So how come you know?

RUBY: Hey, you guys. I have a beautiful plan, let's hide. Everyone hide
before she comes, hide!

TEDDY: No.

RUBY: Why not, hey c'mon Teddy, hide with me.

   (TEDDY ignores her.)

Oh well, I'm gonna hide.

   (RUBY searches for a place to hide.)

HOTEL MAN: Ted, follow her. You can't just be standing there like a bag
of wet sand when Darlene walks in.

   (DARLENE enters.)

DARLENE: Oh dear, what's all this?

RUBY: Surprise, surprise, hey you big fat loser, have a surprise!!

DARLENE: Oh my, oh … this is for me?

TEDDY: Congratulations, Darlene.

DARLENE: Wow …

RUBY: *(To DARLENE.)* Hey, look at the cake, it's hilarious. It looks like
a fuckin' rock.

DARLENE: This is great, I feel like a young girl. I love cake and I love
balloons too, I love them. What pretty colors you've picked, everything
goes so nicely. What a transformation.

HOTEL MAN: You're glowing.

DARLENE: Am I?

HOTEL MAN: So tell us, how does it feel to join the magical land of the employed?

DARLENE: Pretty different. Money might not be everything but it is when you don't have any.

HOTEL MAN: Truer words were never spoken. It's the same problem with love. Money and love will be the death of this century. But who cares, we have a working woman in our midst.

DARLENE: We live in garbage.

HOTEL MAN: And the thrilling thing about that is we get to wear garbage. I can't believe I said that. I have all the time in the world but every minute going by feels like a brick landing on my head. I'm so ungrateful.

TEDDY: Yes, you are. I wish I was dead.

RUBY: It's a party, pussycat, don't get morose. Do you want some more rye? Let's open some scotch, there's lots.

HOTEL MAN: It's not uncommon to wish you were dead. I often wish I was dead and there's nothing particularly wrong with my life.

TEDDY: No there isn't. Stop being so critical.

HOTEL MAN: Are you drunk?

TEDDY: What kind of a question is that? Of course I'm drunk.

HOTEL MAN: I can never tell with you.

TEDDY: Let's have a toast.

HOTEL MAN: Drink as much as you like, just remember who bought it.

RUBY: Hear that Ted, free booze. We'll do anything for free booze. If you like we'll even take off our clothes.

HOTEL MAN: *(To RUBY.)* Don't even think of it.

RUBY: *(To DARLENE.)* You have a card, can I open your card for you? Here—

> *(RUBY opens Darlene's card and hands it to her. DARLENE reads the card.)*

DARLENE: Love may trust but few, always paddle your own canoe ... Congratulations, love and success in your new job you deserve it more than anyone in the world ... Happy Birthday?

TEDDY: *(To DARLENE.)* Learn to trust your friends and I'll write the right thing in the right card next time.

HOTEL MAN: Can you two be angels and fetch some ice, it's sitting in the back room on top of the filing cabinet.

(RUBY and DARLENE exit.)

Darlene is very nervous about this job. She hasn't worked in ages. Her last job was with some landscaping company and it was a total nightmare. She had a hideous encounter with some young boys.

TEDDY: What kind of boys?

HOTEL MAN: Delivery boys, I don't know. What other kind of boys are there? Maybe they weren't boys at all, maybe they were men. But the way the situation was described it all sounded very nasty. I pictured boys. It could have easily been women in fact. There was no mention of boys in the record, so why did I say boys just now?

TEDDY: What happened?

HOTEL MAN: She had a hideous encounter with some people. Nice normal people, who weren't very keen on her. It got so every time the supervisor walked in the room she nearly ran out of the building. But the final straw was the stapler.

TEDDY: Yeah, I heard about the stapler.

HOTEL MAN: She smashed it down onto someone's fingers. They let her go.

TEDDY: It doesn't take much.

HOTEL MAN: Not these days.

TEDDY: I worked in the bush, you know? I bet you didn't know, you didn't know did you? I was a bush cook up in Salmon Arm. There's an awful lot you don't know.

HOTEL MAN: Here, eat some cake, it'll soak up whatever it is you've been pouring down you. You're beginning to resemble Mr. Horowitz, get a grip.

TEDDY: One day we'll all resemble Mr. Horowitz.

HOTEL MAN: Here, eat. Hey you gals, ice, ice ...

(RUBY and DARLENE re-enter.)

RUBY: Hi, here's your ice. Nice, cold, ice.

DARLENE: Heavy and cold just the way ice should be.

RUBY: Frozen solid.

DARLENE: Ted, who said you could cut my cake? I didn't want it cut I wanted to look at it for a while. You wrecked my cake.

TEDDY: This icing tastes like salad dressing. I hate cake.

HOTEL MAN: All right everyone, a toast.

TEDDY: I don't even know where she works. I bet he knows where you work.

DARLENE: Atlas Industrial Carpets. I'm cleaning all those long carpets you see in the malls so you don't break your neck. I'm cleaning them in a gigantic washing machine the size of a bus.

TEDDY: Is it fun?

DARLENE: I don't know.

HOTEL MAN: To a woman who is—

RUBY: A *big fat loser!!*

HOTEL MAN: It's not how I would have put it.

RUBY: I'm kidding. She knows I'm kidding.

HOTEL MAN: Raise your glasses to a woman of proportion, depth, and humility.

TEDDY: Could probably do with less humility and more humanity. I'm not pointing any fingers.

HOTEL MAN: *(To DARLENE.)* The host is prepared and ready for action, what does your heart desire?

TEDDY: How did you get this job?

DARLENE: I got it through the health centre.

TEDDY: Do they have lots of jobs?

DARLENE: No.

TEDDY: Maybe I could get something.

DARLENE: Maybe. Can I have some ice?

TEDDY: Do you think it's worth giving them a call or maybe I should drop in?

DARLENE: Sure.

RUBY: Hey everyone ice! Let's have an ice fight! Ice fight—

HOTEL MAN: *(To RUBY.)* Didn't your parents teach you anything? She doesn't have any life skills. Ice hurts, Ruby, it's cold and hard. Ice hurts.

RUBY: I'm not really going to throw it. I'm just going to sprinkle it around. Hey, career woman, catch this.

(RUBY lobs a handful of ice in DARLENE's direction.)

DARLENE: *(To RUBY.)* Here, stash this in your bra, I mean your brassiere, I mean your bra.

TEDDY: *Aaaahhh*—She put it down my back!

DARLENE: You were getting too excited, I had to take emergency measures.

HOTEL MAN: I'd be further ahead running a daycare centre, at least I'd have a dental plan.

TEDDY: Yes well, I'd be further ahead as a brain surgeon and Ruby would be much happier teaching girls gym.

DARLENE: Ted! He stuck a big chunk down my armpit.

TEDDY: We don't have to worry about Darlene's future, she's the queen of carpet land.

RUBY: Hey, this cools off your boobs.

HOTEL MAN: Keep your pet discoveries to yourself, Ruby.

RUBY: Oh God, he's so repressed. Here, wanna eat some ice? Eat some ice.

HOTEL MAN: Thanks, no.

RUBY: Afraid you're going to get aroused?

HOTEL MAN: No.

TEDDY: Can you catch? Duck!

(RUBY and TEDDY continue to horse around.)

HOTEL MAN: *(To DARLENE.)* You're not like them.

DARLENE: Oh, but I am. You haven't seen me, you don't know—

HOTEL MAN: You don't have to apologize. Stop apologizing. You are the bright light on the horizon. It's something you should celebrate.

DARLENE: I will.

HOTEL MAN: Here I have something for you, it's a talisman.

DARLENE: Oh, a ring. It's somebody's wedding ring, I think. Are wedding rings good luck? I'm not sure.

HOTEL MAN: Don't be silly, take it. I want you to have it.

DARLENE: I can't, it's too much, these diamonds are real. This belonged to someone's wife. I'm not a wife, I've never even come close. Besides I remember reading somewhere the diamond is an incredibly unlucky stone. They bring bad luck and anyway I never wear rings.

HOTEL MAN: Your brand of logic is infectious, but if you don't let me help you, you're going to get slapped.

DARLENE: I'll take care of it for you, but I can't—

HOTEL MAN: Thank you. There, now it's yours. It belongs to you. Keep it, I insist.

DARLENE: It's very pretty, thank you. I'll take good care of it for you.

HOTEL MAN: You don't have to tell anyone. It can be a little secret, *entres nous.*

TEDDY: *(To RUBY.)* Is he holding her hand?

RUBY: I think he was touching it—I definitely saw him touching it. He touched her for sure. She shouldn't let him do that, she really shouldn't.

TEDDY: No, it probably isn't a good idea.

RUBY: Hey you two, stop feeling each other up!

HOTEL MAN: I would keep Ruby at arm's length if I were you. At least until you find your way.

DARLENE: Yes, it's true I'm overwhelmed. People tell me things, there's nothing I can do but listen, you know, so I do, but it's so hard to hear some of it, and then I get so resentful I want to shriek.

HOTEL MAN: Well, you're a bit of a love machine. You've got to learn to keep something for yourself.

DARLENE: I do.

HOTEL MAN: Let me help you. My sweet one. I'll help you, I will.

(He embraces her firmly in his arms. RUBY and TEDDY watch as HOTEL MAN slowly releases DARLENE from his arms.)

RUBY: Darlene?

DARLENE: What?

RUBY: Are you—

DARLENE: Am I what? Am I what?

Scene Eight

(The hotel lobby. HOTEL MAN is reading a newspaper. TEDDY is sitting in the lobby.)

HOTEL MAN: Is today the eighteenth? It is, isn't it?

TEDDY: I guess so.

HOTEL MAN: My uncle Graham shot himself in the head on this day, he'd just turned thirty-eight. I was twelve at the time. I don't know what got into him. He drank like a fish. I adored him. My parents lied through their teeth and kept telling me he'd fallen off his horse. Well at the funeral I got quite a different story but to this day if I ever mention his name they stick to their guns. "Graham. Yes, poor uncle Graham. Trampled by a horse." I'm forty, he was two years younger than I am now. Have you read this article on caterpillar moths?

TEDDY: No, I haven't.

HOTEL MAN: It's just as well, they lead a very unfortunate existence. Do you read newspapers?

TEDDY: No, I have a television. How old was Mr. Horowitz?

HOTEL MAN: I don't know, he could have been any age.

TEDDY: No he couldn't, he could only be the age he was.

HOTEL MAN: He was the crazy uncle no one ever talked about, a genuine eccentric.

TEDDY: Who, Horowitz?

HOTEL MAN: No, Graham. Probably would have fit in quite nicely here, come to think of it. I didn't really know Horowitz, did you?

TEDDY: No but somebody must have.

HOTEL MAN: He was so cut off he lived like an aging movie star. He sort of looked like one.

TEDDY: He had a wife.

HOTEL MAN: Yes, I came across a photograph of the two of them leaning against the hood of a red car. It's amazing what becomes of people.

TEDDY: It's not all you came across.

HOTEL MAN: And so what if it isn't? He had some wonderful things. He must have been something at one time, perhaps the family had money. His shirts were always pressed. He probably ate cardboard.

TEDDY: I never saw him eat anything.

HOTEL MAN: What are you muttering about now?

TEDDY: I don't know.

(Brief pause.)

HOTEL MAN: I went down to the pawn shop, it's just such an unbelievable rip-off. I mean it's really not to be believed, the audacity.

TEDDY: What do you have?

HOTEL MAN: Bits and pieces nothing serious. I'm a collector and I understand why one thing would be valuable and another wouldn't. Still and for all—I've been halfway across the city and back—it's the same story. Bicycle parts, it's all anyone wants to purchase. Fabric, beautiful old bound books, first editions. They just don't get it.

TEDDY: They just don't want it.

HOTEL MAN: You're wrong, there is an absolute market for books, anything well made, but I don't think I'm going to find it in these parts.

TEDDY: Nope, me neither.

HOTEL MAN: I should just get organized and sell it all privately. It could add up to a real little nest egg.

TEDDY: It could but it won't.

HOTEL MAN: And why not?

TEDDY: People don't give a shit about a bunch of moldy old books and scratched up old records. Everybody wants the same thing, everybody wants a new VCR. If you want to look at moldy books and scratchy records you go to the Sally Ann and look at all the moldy things. Everything costs ten cents or a buck or something and still nobody wants it. What do you got, do you know?

HOTEL MAN: Not exactly.

TEDDY: See, you don't even know, you're just babbling.

HOTEL MAN: I'm not.

TEDDY: You are so.

HOTEL MAN: Well, I'm sure something will come of it. I've got a good feeling about it and I'm going to pursue it

TEDDY: It's a great idea, I'm sure you will.

(HOTEL MAN reads from his newspaper.)

HOTEL MAN: According to Henri Farbre, the caterpillar moths travel in hundreds, one behind the other, attached by minute threads of silk they spin out of their bellies. It would seem they are obsessed and will not deviate from the invisible silken threads they attach to one another like umbilical cords. Their limited senses and inability to strike out in any other direction render them imbecilic. They will freeze, starve and march steadily and silently into oncoming traffic rather than embark on any alternate plan or path even when one is set before them. Are you listening to this?

TEDDY: Who's Henri Farbre?

HOTEL MAN: A leading entomologist from France.

TEDDY: Entomologist?

HOTEL MAN: A person devoted to the study of insects. I should invite Henry down here for a weekend of research, his head would spin off.

TEDDY: So you don't know how he died?

HOTEL MAN: Graham? He suicided, I told you.

TEDDY: No, Horowitz.

HOTEL MAN: No, I don't. Do you?

TEDDY: How he ended up? I have some ideas.

HOTEL MAN: You didn't even know him.

TEDDY: I didn't want to know him, he was gonna kick.

HOTEL MAN: Well, your instincts are good, he did.

TEDDY: He had a band under his neck, like a band of—it wasn't the same

color as the rest of his head. It was like a stripe but no it was more like—
it wasn't like anything, it was a band.

HOTEL MAN: So.

TEDDY: He'd catch me staring at his band so I'd wave at him so it was
like I wasn't staring it was like I was waving, but waving made it worse.

HOTEL MAN: Oh yes, waving makes it unbearable.

TEDDY: He wasn't really sick, he wasn't really old either.

HOTEL MAN: No but he was exhausted and his exhaustion was a kind of
disease, really. It spread out over every part of him. Even his clothes
looked ready to keel over.

TEDDY: But he knew something was wrong, he must have.

HOTEL MAN: Yes but Horowitz never asked for help, never. He didn't
know how. It went completely against his upbringing and that did him
in as much as anything in the end. These last few years must have been
quite joyless.

TEDDY: He did things, he was all right.

HOTEL MAN: He read and walked, he was disciplined. It was impressive,
still, Horowitz was a hermit.

TEDDY: Maybe he was a happy hermit.

HOTEL MAN: If you insist. What will I do with my collection if I can't
sell it.

TEDDY: Keep it.

HOTEL MAN: You know what I think would be fun? Wrapping everything up in paper, long pieces of brown butcher paper and then storing
it all away and looking at it in twenty years to see if it means anything.

TEDDY: Yeah well, you'll be here in twenty years. You and your bundles,
you'll both be here.

Scene Nine

*(Teddy's room, the following week. RUBY is coaxing TEDDY to
drink powdered health shakes, mixed from a can with water.)*

TEDDY: It tastes like chalk. Have you ever drunk chalk?

RUBY: C'mon Teddy, don't be stubborn, drink your Ensure. It's full of
vitamins and calories.

TEDDY: Have you ever tried it? It's awful.

RUBY: Who cares, just down it. If you can drink aftershave you can drink
Ensure.

TEDDY: Try it if you don't believe me.

RUBY: I hate it when you get like this, don't be an idiot! Drink your health-shake, Teddy. I don't care what it tastes like, you have to gain some weight.

TEDDY: Put it in the fridge, I'll drink it later.

RUBY: Now I understand why mothers murder their children and leave their bodies in empty parking lots. Drink your Ensure, Ted.

TEDDY: I can't.

RUBY: Yes you can! Of course you can, you're just trying to piss me off. Drink it!

TEDDY: Leave me alone.

RUBY: Why are you doing this to me, why?

TEDDY: I'm not doing anything to anyone. I don't have to listen to you, you're crazy. You and Darlene are crazy. I'm not crazy.

RUBY: I'm crazy because all the nice, sane people I've ever known are weak-kneed, passive-aggressive alcoholics, who make everybody go nuts for them.

TEDDY: You were nuts long before you met me.

RUBY: Yeah, well don't forget who got you off the street, drunk boy.

TEDDY: I haven't, Prozac girl.

RUBY: You're starving to death. I swear to God, Teddy if you don't drink these health shakes I'm going to strangle you.

TEDDY: I said I would.

RUBY: I want to see you drink at least one.

TEDDY: You drink one. I'll drink one if you drink one.

RUBY: Hey this isn't so bad, it's vanilla. It tastes almost exactly like vanilla.

TEDDY: It's like licking drywall. You really are crazy.

RUBY: I'll drink the vanilla, you drink the chocolate. You need nourishment.

TEDDY: No you don't, I've eaten very little over the years. Very few people die from lack of nourishment, the big killer is stress.

RUBY: Here, now you finish this tiny bit.

TEDDY: You drooled in it. I'm not drinking your backwash.

RUBY: I didn't drool, I took one lousy sip.

TEDDY: It's half empty, you may as well finish it.

RUBY: I'll finish this one but you have to drink the rest. You know that dress Darlene wears, the one with the buttons? Well, every time she wears that dress we get into a fight.

TEDDY: She's got a lot on her plate right now.

RUBY: Believe me, nobody's more proud of her than I am. I think the job is the best thing for her but I don't know, I think she's starting to resent me.

TEDDY: No, I don't think so.

RUBY: She thinks that bastard's her friend, but he's not. I'm her friend for Christ's sake, he's not her friend at all.

TEDDY: He's got a soft spot for her.

RUBY: No he doesn't, he's brainwashing her so she won't be my friend. I hope she doesn't turn into a snobby bitch because of this job.

TEDDY: She won't.

RUBY: Oh yeah, well she passed me in the hall yesterday and said, "You stink, Ruby," for no reason. Can you believe it? She walked right past me and said, "You stink." It made me furious. I was almost in tears but I thought, fuck her. So I grabbed her purse and I flushed it down the toilet.

TEDDY: I know, she told me everything dissolved on the bottom of her purse.

RUBY: It's his fault, he's turning her against me. Why is she so impressed by what he thinks? Christ, people are weak.

TEDDY: I'm not weak.

RUBY: No you're great, you just have to stop drinking and start eating and then you'll be perfect. Darlene's getting pretty weak. If she doesn't realize we're her friends she's lost.

TEDDY: He thinks about some very weird things.

RUBY: No kidding, him and his list. What the hell is he doing here, has he ever thought of that?

TEDDY: Who cares, he's a weird man with a room full of crap, it's complete crap. Nobody cares about the stuff he cares about, nobody.

RUBY: Darlene cares, she listens to him.

TEDDY: Darlene listens to everybody, she lets everybody bleed all over her.

RUBY: Do you really think this mat-washing, scrubbing, whatever the hell she does, is going to pan out? I'm not a negative person but I've got my doubts.

TEDDY: Yesterday she told the guy at Mr. Submarine he was a genius. It's not right. She's doing the same thing with Hotel Man. He's getting the wrong idea.

RUBY: Darlene knows exactly what she's doing, she's a goddamn fence sitter.

(TEDDY takes a sip of his health shake.)

TEDDY: Did we really buy this?

RUBY: I didn't buy them, you did. I bought lipstick.

TEDDY: It's awful. I knew it was going to be awful too. How much did I buy?

RUBY: The whole carton. You carried it on your head, don't you remember?

TEDDY: I didn't want to buy them, why do I do that? I bought razors, where are my razors?

RUBY: You didn't buy razors, you bought health shakes.

TEDDY: Do we have any money left?

RUBY: No, you spent it all on Ensure.

TEDDY: Why didn't you stop me?

RUBY: I tried but then you puked up your Samosa in front of Cotton Ginny, the sales clerk came out and I just gave up.

TEDDY: The samosa I remember, the sales clerk I remember. Fuck her.

RUBY: I almost pissed my pants, I can never tell when you're gonna go down. One minute you look like Jackie Kennedy stepping off the airplane and then wham!! Two seconds later, you're flat on your face, spitting up samosa.

TEDDY: She was a cow.

RUBY: We are a very distinct pair; when we walk down the street people take notice.

TEDDY: Yeah, they take notice all right.

RUBY: Well, we're not dull, no one can say that about us. At least we're not puffed wheat for Christ's sake.

TEDDY: Puffed wheat?

RUBY: It came in a big clear plastic bag. It was the dullest cereal ever made in the history of cereal, it was so dull they banned it.

TEDDY: Good, I can't buy it.

RUBY: At least we're not that. We're not dull. We are exotic.

TEDDY: We are fruit loops.

RUBY: Yes, exactly.

TEDDY: Colorful, a little strange-looking, full of preservatives, not very healthy.

RUBY: What's Hotel Man?

TEDDY: Captain Crunch.

RUBY: No he's Count Chocula.

TEDDY: Hey what about Horowitz?

RUBY: Horowitz, I dunno—

TEDDY: Life.

RUBY: Life?

TEDDY: It was a joke.

    (DARLENE enters.)

DARLENE: Hi guys.

TEDDY: *(To DARLENE.)* Hi guys.

DARLENE: *(To TEDDY.)* What? I said, hello.

TEDDY: Hello. I said, "Hello," back.

DARLENE: Look if anyone's hungry I bought a roasted chicken. I bought two, there's lots, and potato salad and buns. It's a lot of food and there's no way I can eat it, so ...

    (RUBY and TEDDY are silent.)

It's roasted chicken.

RUBY: *(To DARLENE.)* Yeah, okay, maybe later. We'll have some later, you go ahead.

DARLENE: I don't want to be left alone downstairs with him anymore. I want someone to come with me.

TEDDY: So stay here.

DARLENE: I told him I'd eat dinner with him.

TEDDY: So go.

DARLENE: Can't you come?

TEDDY: No.

DARLENE: Why not?

TEDDY: Because he'll start telling me about his uncle again.

RUBY: Go ahead Darlene, it's no big deal. Go eat your potato salad.

TEDDY: *(To RUBY.)* Chicken.

RUBY: And potato salad.

TEDDY: Chicken and potato salad.

RUBY: I know, that's what I said.

TEDDY: I thought you said something else.

DARLENE: I don't want to go alone.

RUBY: *(To DARLENE.)* For Christ's sake go, already, you won't be alone!

TEDDY: Hey, what's Darlene?

RUBY: What?

TEDDY: Cereal. Think about it.

DARLENE: What's Darlene, what?

RUBY: Hold on ... let me figure it out ... I know—

TEDDY: She's—

RUBY: Grape Nuts!!

TEDDY: Grape Nuts!!

DARLENE: I'm what? *(Beat.)* Whatever.

>   *(DARLENE exits.)*

TEDDY: Guess you had to be there.

RUBY: Bye, Grape Nuts. Go eat your chicken!

Scene Ten

>   *(The hotel lobby. HOTEL MAN is seated behind the desk. RUBY tries to slip past him unnoticed. He is waiting for her.)*

HOTEL MAN: Ruby, where are you going?

RUBY: Hi! I'm going upstairs—

HOTEL MAN: I'd like to have a word with you.

RUBY: Okay, great. I'll be back in a second, I have to see Teddy for a sec—

HOTEL MAN: I need to speak to you now, it's important.

RUBY: Oh, sure, okay, now? Right now eh, it can't wait a minute?

HOTEL MAN: No, I'm afraid not. Can you come here?

RUBY: Sure, what is it?

HOTEL MAN: I'm concerned—

RUBY: Concerned about what?

HOTEL MAN: Don't interrupt, let me finish. I'm concerned with how you're getting on.

RUBY: Oh, I'm great. I'm happy—

HOTEL MAN: I'm not convinced actually. Not that you have to convince me, but it is a problem.

RUBY: What's the problem? I don't see any problem.

HOTEL MAN: That in itself is part of the problem.

RUBY: What do you mean? I haven't done anything.

HOTEL MAN: Can I give you a small piece of advice?

RUBY: Sure, what?

HOTEL MAN: Getting upset won't help.

RUBY: Who's upset—I'm not upset!

HOTEL MAN: Good, because I need you to hear what I have to say to you. *(Beat.)* I don't think it's working out for you here.

RUBY: What? Of course it is. It's working out perfectly.

HOTEL MAN: I've logged another complaint.

RUBY: From who, who is it?

HOTEL MAN: Someone—

RUBY: Can you please tell me who the hell "someone" is?

HOTEL MAN: Someone isn't asking you to leave, I am. There are three different complaints from three different people.

RUBY: The toilets don't flush and the goddamn ceiling is going to come crashing down on our heads any minute, can someone complain about that?

HOTEL MAN: The toilets and the ceilings are a symptom of the city. You live in a city where the rent is high. You have no money and you will never have money.

RUBY: Symptoms my ass, this is kangaroo court!

HOTEL MAN: Part of the reason you're here is because I let you stay here.

RUBY: I pay money—I pay all my money to live here, this is my home.

HOTEL MAN: Perhaps it's time you started looking for a new one.

RUBY: I have friends, my friends won't let you do this to me.

HOTEL MAN: It's not your friends I have a problem with, it's you.

RUBY: So what, I have a problem with you too!

HOTEL MAN: I rest my case.

RUBY: I know exactly what's going on. You're trying to screw me into a corner. What if I complain?

HOTEL MAN: You're not a popular girl these days; to be frank, you're disliked.

RUBY: That's a lie.

HOTEL MAN: It's not. I've warned you, even your friends have warned you.

RUBY: I want to see this list.

HOTEL MAN: This isn't about what you want.

RUBY: Darlene hates your guts.

HOTEL MAN: Maybe she does, I doubt it. Hate is a very strong word.

RUBY: Liar, I hate you! And so does Darlene and so does Teddy and so does everyone. We hate you! You stare at my tits and you steal from the dead, can I put that on your list?

HOTEL MAN: Certainly, you can write it in next to the last entry.

(*He takes out the scribbler and spreads it out for RUBY to see.*)

RUBY: Darlene complained about me? Why did Darlene complain about me, why?

HOTEL MAN: I don't know, she wouldn't say.

Scene Eleven

(*The hotel lobby, early evening the same day. DARLENE enters with fresh strawberries.*)

DARLENE: Have some strawberries, I brought them for you.

HOTEL MAN: Strawberries, how wonderful. Fresh fruit is a true respite from this life.

DARLENE: Oh, yes. My doctor says I need positive reinforcement and a stable environment.

HOTEL MAN: Who doesn't.

DARLENE: A lot of my problems are not being able to have my own finances but I'm going to make it. I'm going to make it out there.

HOTEL MAN: So you're going to stick with it then, excellent.

DARLENE: I've made it before, I can make it happen again.

HOTEL MAN: You're looking a bit breathless, is everything all right?

DARLENE: I think so.

HOTEL MAN: I worry about you. You will keep it won't you.

DARLENE: My job, I don't know. I'll try.

HOTEL MAN: Promise me.

DARLENE: It's a job, no guarantees.

HOTEL MAN: Do the carpet people know anything about your employment history?

DARLENE: No. My doctor says it's nobody's business.

HOTEL MAN: Your doctor sounds like an odd duck.

DARLENE: You're sweating like a horse. What have you been doing all afternoon?

HOTEL MAN: It hasn't exactly been a breeze.

DARLENE: Did Teddy get sick?

HOTEL MAN: No, nothing like that, Teddy's fine. He's fine.

DARLENE: Good, I'm always expecting the—

HOTEL MAN: Where did you find these strawberries? They taste like penicillin.

DARLENE: Are they moldy?

HOTEL MAN: A little, yes.

DARLENE: Are you all right?

HOTEL MAN: Things just got a little out of hand and it's a bit complicated at the moment. I'm not happy, well it's been going on and on and today it came to a head, it was bound to. I'm not ready just this minute to go into details. As you can see it's put me in a foul mood. I don't mean to take it out on you but—

DARLENE: What—

HOTEL MAN: It's Ruby, she's going. She's out.

DARLENE: Ruby out? What, out where?

HOTEL MAN: I don't know that's entirely up to her.

DARLENE: Where is she?

HOTEL MAN: Upstairs.

DARLENE: What happened?

HOTEL MAN: Nothing.

DARLENE: What did you say to her?

HOTEL MAN: Not much—anyway I'm not getting into it now.

DARLENE: She doesn't have anywhere to go.

HOTEL MAN: It has nothing to do with me.

DARLENE: But she really doesn't have—

HOTEL MAN: She'll have to arrange something with her social worker.

DARLENE: I think—

HOTEL MAN: Darlene, don't start. Don't start with me!

(Silence.)

I want you to think about your own happiness. Are you crying?

DARLENE: I'm the happiest person I know.

HOTEL MAN: But what does that mean.

DARLENE: My head's throbbing, I don't understand any of this ... does your head ever throb?

HOTEL MAN: Not that I'm aware of.

DARLENE: It feels like all the blood in my body is rushing into my brain. It comes gushing in and then everything smells like steel. It's just like right before you puke, only instead of sick, you're waiting for all the blood.

HOTEL MAN: Are you going to collapse?

DARLENE: No, I'm going to stand very still ... The trick is to not move ... to be still.

HOTEL MAN: Are you going to bleed?

DARLENE: No.

HOTEL MAN: What's that sound?

DARLENE: My teeth.

HOTEL MAN: You're shaking, I've upset you. I'm sorry, I should never have brought all this up.

DARLENE: Don't touch my back. People are always touching my back and I never know what to do, never.

HOTEL MAN: You're so tense, just let me—

DARLENE: No, don't.

HOTEL MAN: Calm down, relax. Just breathe and—

DARLENE: I'll break something. Don't touch me, I'll break something.

HOTEL MAN: I'm sorry.

DARLENE: What did you do with my cake, you know I didn't get a single bite of cake.

HOTEL MAN: You look like you're about to unravel, go to bed and rest immediately.

(DARLENE goes to exit, then stops and turns.)

DARLENE: But I really got a kick out of the card because my mum used to say that. Did you know? No, you couldn't know, how could you know. Love may trust but few always paddle your own canoe. It was one of her whaddya call it, expressions? Yeah, it was one of her expressions.

(DARLENE exits.)

Scene Twelve

(Darlene's room. DARLENE has locked herself in the bathroom. TEDDY is kneeling next to a pile of damp towels and mops up water in front of the door.)

TEDDY: You're making a hell of a mess for someone who says she wants to be left alone. Darlene, I'm running out of towels?

(Silence.)

Darlene, the floor is wet?

(Silence.)

You have to keep talking to me. I'm not going to sit here cleaning a great big mess if you won't even talk to me.

DARLENE: *(From behind the closed door.)* Why don't you talk to me and I'll answer, seeing how I have nothing to say and you have so much on your mind.

TEDDY: You've been in there a long time.

DARLENE: Have I?

TEDDY: Yes, you have.

DARLENE: How long?

TEDDY: Too long.

DARLENE: How long is too long?

TEDDY: Will you please stop splashing and spilling water around, it's everywhere.

DARLENE: I can't help it, it's plugged.

TEDDY: What's plugged, plugged with what?

DARLENE: It's plugged somehow and it won't unplug.

TEDDY: Plugged with what?

DARLENE: It's plugged or stuck or something.

TEDDY: Darlene?

DARLENE: It looks like a little waterfall. It's nice, I like it.

TEDDY: It what?

DARLENE: It's very refreshing and do you know what else?

TEDDY: No, what else?

DARLENE: All these ugly rust stains on the bottom of the bathroom floor? I'm pretending they're coral rocks.

TEDDY: But they're not coral rocks, they're rust stains.

DARLENE: I know, I'm pretending.

> *(Silence.)*

The faucet is a—

TEDDY: Darlene!

DARLENE: Diamond frog.

TEDDY: Darlene, stop it!

DARLENE: I'm just pretending.

TEDDY: Stop pretending!

DARLENE: It's a game.

TEDDY: It's a stupid game! It's stupid, stop it, it's a faucet. You're in the bathroom and you're making a fucking mess!

> *(Silence.)*

Darlene, I want you to get out of the bathroom. You've been in there too long. I want you to stop thinking about coral rocks and diamond frogs, it's bullshit. You know it's bullshit, so stop it.

> *(Silence.)*

Will you answer me? It's so shitty you won't even answer me.

> *(Silence.)*

It's bullshit, but you do what you want. You always have.

> *(RUBY enters.)*

Leave her alone.

RUBY: Where is she?

TEDDY: In the bathroom.

RUBY: Is she all right.

TEDDY: The door's locked, just leave her.

RUBY: She went out this morning at about six. She's been up all night. I knocked on her door but she wouldn't answer.

TEDDY: Don't argue with her and don't tell her she's crazy.

RUBY: Teddy, I just had a brainstorm. Why don't I give her some of my Prozac, it'll calm her down.

> *(RUBY knocks on the bathroom door.)*

I take Prozac and beer, it works perfectly. Darlene, pussycat, it's me. How are you doing in there? Would you like some Prozac, pussycat? Some nice Prozac and some nice beer. Hey, pussycat?

TEDDY: Leave her, Ruby.

RUBY: What?

TEDDY: I mean it, leave her alone.

(HOTEL MAN knocks, then enters.)

HOTEL MAN: What's going on up here?

TEDDY: Nothing.

HOTEL MAN: What are those?

TEDDY: What are what?

HOTEL MAN: Those?

TEDDY: That?

HOTEL MAN: Yes, that.

TEDDY: That's towels. Towels and shirts.

HOTEL MAN: Are you washing towels?

TEDDY: And shirts.

HOTEL MAN: About three minutes ago I was nearly crushed to death by a few hundred pounds of ceiling.

TEDDY: Ceiling?

HOTEL MAN: Yes, ceiling.

TEDDY: The whole ceiling?

HOTEL MAN: A good portion of it is now sitting on the floor drenched in water.

TEDDY: I told you I was washing shirts and towels. It leaks, you know.

HOTEL MAN: What leaks?

TEDDY: The bathtub. I had to refill it about five times. If there's any damage to the ceiling we would pay the full price of course, if we did any damage.

HOTEL MAN: You don't have any money.

TEDDY: Deduct it from our rent.

HOTEL MAN: It's maddening, you live in a fog. I can't penetrate the fog you all live in, it's too thick.

TEDDY: In my room is an antique teapot. Turn of the century, hand painted, gold leaf, birds ... take it.

HOTEL MAN: Birds of paradise. I think I remember seeing it but who knows what it's worth if anything.

TEDDY: I can show you, it's in my room.

RUBY: Yeah Ted, show him your teapot.

HOTEL MAN: *(To TEDDY.)* You don't know how to participate in your own life. Did you know that about yourself.

(The bathroom door swings open and DARLENE appears. She is fully dressed, but her clothes are drenched in water.)

DARLENE: I was nominated to be the valedictorian of my high school. There were two thousand kids at that high school and I was one of the nominees. They did an IQ test. I think those tests are for the birds but anyway mine was high, over 150. I didn't win. Mine was the best speech, everyone said so, but I failed Physics in the first semester and Mr. Stein said the valedictorian can't fail Physics. "The valedictorian has to be more even keel," is what he said. It doesn't matter, it really doesn't. I have worked hard. I have worked all my life. I've watched and learned things, things you wouldn't imagine. You have to have an eye, you have to see, I do. I'm lucky, I learn fast, but you can't rely on natural ability. You have to develop a skill. Mat washing is a skill, you know, it takes practice. People's heels leave marks and gouges in the weave. I unroll every single mat and assess the damage. The damage depends on the traffic. Where are these mats coming from and where will they go to? I have to know. I have to decide. All my life all I ever wanted to do was learn and I will. I will practice and practice and practice my mat washing until I am the best and most dedicated mat washer there is. I just want to be able to do it. I want to do it well. I will, you'll see. My mats, my mats are going to shine and float in the sun.

HOTEL MAN: Why are you deliberately destructive to my hotel?

TEDDY: *(To RUBY.)* "My hotel." It's not his hotel.

HOTEL MAN: I can't permit any of you to destroy the property. I'm calling the police.

RUBY: Darlene, he's gonna call the cops.

DARLENE: He doesn't know cops. Jerry knows cops this guy doesn't know anybody.

TEDDY: He knows a few cab drivers.

DARLENE: Go ahead call the police. Call the doctor, call the telephone company. Call Sprint Canada. Call Candice Bergen. Call whoever you like. I'm not in, take a message.

HOTEL MAN: Unbelievable.

DARLENE: Don't give this man your teapot, I forbid you. It's the only thing he has.

RUBY: Pussycat, your prescription is ready.

DARLENE: No rush, I'll get it Monday.

RUBY: We can get it now, it's ready now.

DARLENE: I don't want it now.

RUBY: Don't you want your pills, pussycat?

DARLENE: No they're too expensive, and anyway, they make me suicidal.

(DARLENE exits.)

HOTEL MAN: I run a hotel full of dead people.

Scene Thirteen

(The hotel lobby, a day and a half later. HOTEL MAN is standing in the doorway of the lobby entrance.)

HOTEL MAN: What is he trying to accomplish?

DARLENE: Who?

HOTEL MAN: Teddy.

DARLENE: I don't know, I haven't been paying attention.

HOTEL MAN: It's fascinating, he lives on another planet. The fog rolls in and carries him off. He looks so puzzled and hurt. Darlene, go and tell him.

DARLENE: Go and tell him what?

HOTEL MAN: Something, you have to say something.

DARLENE: About what?

HOTEL MAN: It's hot out there.

DARLENE: Where is he?

HOTEL MAN: Standing in the middle of the street with sweat pouring down his chest trying to hail a cab. None of them will stop, he's half dressed.

DARLENE: I hope he's not getting sick.

HOTEL MAN: I've got to go check on the towels, they should be dry by now. Watch him, see he doesn't get run over.

(HOTEL MAN exits, DARLENE goes to the doorway.)

DARLENE: Teddy, get in here now. Get in the shade or you'll pass out like you did before!

(DARLENE moves away from the door. TEDDY enters.)

TEDDY: They don't see me.

DARLENE: Who?

TEDDY: The drivers—they don't look or they won't look, I don't know.

DARLENE: Oh, never mind them.

TEDDY: Doesn't matter either way really, does it. I mean it amounts to about the same thing in the end, doesn't it?

DARLENE: What?

TEDDY: Visibility.

DARLENE: I'm not sure what you mean.

TEDDY: A person can see you or he can't, right? You're there or you're not, right?

DARLENE: One would hope.

TEDDY: They won't stop for me. It makes me want to scream but it makes me want to laugh too. I couldn't decide to scream or laugh so I came back in.

DARLENE: You aren't even wearing any shoes. Nobody will stop if you're in bare feet. You're not getting sick, are you?

TEDDY: No.

(HOTEL MAN enters with clean towels.)

DARLENE: I could get Jerry to drive you to hospital.

TEDDY: I haven't seen Jerry around.

DARLENE: Oh, he's around.

TEDDY: Well, I didn't see him and he didn't see me either.

DARLENE: Don't be a fool, he'd drive you anywhere.

HOTEL MAN: Is Ruby packed?

DARLENE: She packed last night.

TEDDY: I'm getting sick.

HOTEL MAN: I can get you a taxi.

TEDDY: No, it's okay. You fold your towels.

HOTEL MAN: It would take about two minutes.

TEDDY: No!! No … no. I don't want one of your taxis.

HOTEL MAN: They won't stop for you.

TEDDY: I'll get my own taxi, my own way. I can get a taxi.

(TEDDY rushes out.)

(Off.) Hey taxi! Taxi—

DARLENE: Now look what you've done.

HOTEL MAN: He won't go far.

(RUBY enters.)

DARLENE: You don't really have to leave, it's not like he's going to force you out. He won't. You could stay here I know you could.

RUBY: It's too late now. It's done. I'm going.

DARLENE: Where?

RUBY: I'm going to see my father. He lives thousands of miles away. He hasn't seen me in seven years but he'll see me now. He doesn't have a choice, does he? I don't have any money and I don't have anywhere to live. I may as well take a vacation. Are you staying?

DARLENE: Oh, I'll be here unless of course I have an epiphany. In which case I'll be here anyway.

RUBY: I just want to make sure I can always find you.

DARLENE: I'm not hard to find. I'll probably be fast asleep when you do find me. If I am you can wake me up. You have my permission in advance to wake up the sleeping woman.

RUBY: Maybe my dad won't want to see me, he might not.

DARLENE: Visiting is hard, I find letters are best.

RUBY: Who knows, maybe he will and you'll never see me again.

DARLENE: I don't have any ideas about tomorrow or the day after. I don't know. If you're ready I'll walk you to the bus terminal.

RUBY: No don't—I'll be fine on my own.

DARLENE: You want to go alone?

RUBY: Yes, it's better if I'm alone. I can concentrate on my bus ride.

(HOTEL MAN has been standing in the doorway half-watching TEDDY, half-listening to the women. He enters fully.)

RUBY: No ceiling, no phone, your glory days are over—just kidding.

HOTEL MAN: Parents can be tricky, I'm sure yours are no exception. Don't forget Teddy, he's outside.

RUBY: I won't forget Teddy, I won't forget anything.

DARLENE: Go on then, hurry up catch your bus. I'm going to catch some sleep.

(DARLENE moves to embrace RUBY.)

RUBY: Oh God, please don't hug me—I want to leave in one piece.

DARLENE: Okay, go ahead. Good-bye, Ruby.

RUBY: Bye, Pussycat.

(RUBY exits. Silence.

TEDDY enters. They all look to one another. Silence.

The end.)

Charming & Rose:
True Love

by
Kelley Jo Burke

The première production of *Charming and Rose: True Love* was produced by Boomer Co. of Regina and opened in Regina, Saskatchewan on July 6, 1992 at the Globe Theatre with the following cast:

ROSE	Burgundy Cole
CHARMING	Rick Hughes
MELISANDE	Susan Martin Pavelick

Directed by Kelly Handarek
Stage Manager: Danni Phillipson
Costumer: Denise Ketcheson
Set Designer, Builder and Graphic Artist: George Fathers
Board Operator and House Manager: Teresa Horne

A later production at the Theatre Centre in Toronto ran from October 12 to 31, 1993 and featured the following cast and crew:

ROSE	Kristina Nicoll
CHARMING	Rick Roberts
MELISANDE	Djanet Sears

Produced by Jennifer Stein
Directed by Kate Lushington
Set and Costume Design by Astrid Janson
Lighting Design by Elizabeth Asselstine
Sound Design and Original Music by Boko Suzuki
Stage Manager: Cheryl Francis
Film Producer: Jane Thompson
Film Researcher: Francine Zuckerman

Acknowledgements

The playwright gratefully acknowledges the support of the City of Regina, the Saskatchewan Arts Board and the Saskatchewan Playwrights Centre, and Nightwood Theatre's Groundswell Festival.

Characters

ROSE: A wolf in princess's clothing.

CHARMING: A handsome and eligible prince.

MELISANDE: A professional fairy godmother.

(The play opens with music playing on a harpsichord, fading out with the call of wolves. The play takes place in a tower. There is a bed, a table and two chairs, and one window. A dress stands by itself—a construct of wire and fabric.

ROSE sits on her bed, wrapped in her very long hair. She is humming the melody heard at the play's opening like a lullaby. CHARMING is lying on the floor. She stares at him. She moves towards him. A change in lighting indicates ROSE is now in a memory. He stands, and suddenly they are struggling. She struggles viciously with him, biting and scratching, until finally, he has her arms pinned behind her. He forces her to him, pressing her up his chest, and kisses her. She bites him. He yells, pulling back, and then tries again. She continues to fight, but begins to respond. As she relaxes, he slowly releases one arm, which creeps up his back. He holds onto the other, as the kiss becomes extremely passionate. She pulls back, and looks at him; he freezes. She goes back to the bed. He sinks back down to his former position on the floor. The lights retirn to normal and ROSE is back in the present—this effect is used throughout the play to distinguish between scenes in the present and memory. Just as CHARMING is almost prone, ROSE bounds back, and replays the memory, entering it a little later than the first time and withdrawing earlier in the kiss. This time she stays as he lays back down. Crouching over him, she prods him slightly with her foot, passes her hands over his hair, face. Shivering, she retreats into her hair.

There's a clatter at the window. ROSE leaps beside the window, poised to attack whoever comes through.

Various paraphernalia is sticking on the window frame as MELISANDE tries to enter the tower. She is obviously making some effort to float, or light, or do something delicate and graceful, and it just isn't working out.)

MELISANDE: Shit.

(She clambers in.)

ROSE: It's you.

MELISANDE: You girls have become so jaded. Used to be, you flew in someone's window, you got a reaction. A "Fairy Godmother, thank heavens you've come," or "Bless my soul, how can such wonders be?" or—

ROSE: Do you want tea, Auntie Mel?

MELISANDE: Or even a nice warm, "Do you want tea, Auntie Mel, you dear old supernatural thing you. Hard flight?"

ROSE: If you want tea, you're going to have to bring it in yourself.

MELISANDE: *(Making a magical gesture.)* Behind the bed—I think.

> *(ROSE fetches out the tea tray, and sets it on the table.)*

> *(Remonstrating.)* Rose. Etiquette.

> *(Pause.)*

ROSE: May I pour you a cup?

MELISANDE: You may.

> *(ROSE begins to pour. She sniffs the cup.)*

ROSE: Tea?

MELISANDE: Tea is a state of mind. Gin *(She sips.)* is a state of grace.

ROSE: You're too late, you know.

MELISANDE: You haven't had the baby yet, have you? I just got your letter a day or so ago *(Sipping.)* or at least a week or so ago, and unless you've figured out how to avoid nearly a year of the most absurdly undignified discomfort Nature could contrive on one of her particularly vindictive days, *(Sipping again.)* you haven't had the baby yet.

ROSE: No … I haven't had the baby yet.

MELISANDE: Then what's wrong? You look like a snuffed candle, dear.

ROSE: Guess.

MELISANDE: *(Looking around in a circle.)* You're still living in this stupid evocation of every man's dream erection?

> *(ROSE shakes her head.)*

Your bed needs making. Oh.

> *(She spots CHARMING. She takes a large sip.)*

Oh dear.

ROSE: Right—

MELISANDE: Charming? It is Charming, isn't it?

ROSE: Of course it's Charming. Who else would it be, when I haven't seen another living soul in two years but Charming?

MELISANDE: Living soul would be overstating the case.

ROSE: You didn't know this had happened?

MELISANDE: I'm magic, dear, not omniscient. Such a handsome boy, too. I suspect you need some of my tea.

(*ROSE shakes her head.*)

Three years among humans, and you still don't drink? Sweetie, by now, I'd think you wouldn't be doing much else. Bottom's up.

ROSE: (*Drinking.*) Charming's dead, Auntie Mel.

MELISANDE: I can see that, dear. Take another sip.

ROSE: It burns.

MELISANDE: Always does if you put it on top of crying.

ROSE: It hurts.

MELISANDE: I can't do a thing about that, honey.

ROSE: Why not?

MELISANDE: Resurrection's not my line either, dear.

ROSE: Then what good are you? I'm making a wish, Fairy Godmother ... that is your line, isn't it? I'm wishing that Charming wasn't dead.

MELISANDE: Are you, Rose? Then why'd you kill him?

ROSE: (*Sinking down, staring ahead, and beginning to rock.*) Jesus motherfucking Christ.

MELISANDE: I see your vocabulary has expanded.

ROSE: Princesses don't swear. Princesses don't burp. Princesses don't pass wind, sweat, shit, zit, or drool.

MELISANDE: Princesses don't appear to swear, burp, et cetera, et cetera. I never could get you to grasp the finer points of that principle.

ROSE: What's the difference?

MELISANDE: The difference is that everyone, including princesses, does all of those things. Otherwise they would swell, strain, and eventually erupt, sending a geyser of unexcreted bodily and psychic waste up to heaven, which would then rain down on the horrified faces of those unfortunate enough to be in the vicinity. However, princesses manage to conceal this obvious fact. That's what gives them their edge. They appear. They deceive. They deceive others. Not themselves. But then deception in its entirety eluded you.

ROSE: I'm not a real princess—

MELISANDE: You're the daughter of a king and queen.

ROSE: Who didn't want me.

MELISANDE: That's not true. Your mother wanted you terribly. Dorothea's last thoughts were of you. (*Pause.*) She called out to me, as they laid you in her arms, and the blood gouted out of her, and she made her wish for you ... let her be beautiful ... that sweet, gorgeous, stunningly stupid creature. She'd been married to Harold for twelve years, and all she could think to ask for you were good cheekbones. It was her right ... she was one of mine, after all.

ROSE: Yours don't seem to do too well.

MELISANDE: I don't make the wishes, dear. I only grant them. Dorothea's mother could have wished her the strength to survive that ghastly birth. Or the good sense to avoid Harold. I did better by you, Rose. Your mother wished you lovely. And by god, you are. I do good work. But I wished you smart. And White Paws, she wished you strong. All those mothers. Poor child. Having one mother's hard enough. You had three.

ROSE: White Paws was Mother. You were—

MELISANDE: Your dear old Auntie Mel, without whom you would not be who you are today.

(ROSE stares at her for a minute.)

ROSE: I didn't know the other—

MELISANDE: It's all right. I don't think anyone knew Dorothea. Least of all Harold. And you didn't miss a thing not knowing Harold. *(Smiling mysteriously.)* I wonder how things are going with Harold.

ROSE: Do you think he's still alive?

MELISANDE: Oh, I hope so. I chose syphilis because it takes such a long time.

(MELISANDE enters a memory.)

There's a place, in the forest, where the exposure of infants is traditionally carried out.

(The sound of a baby crying is heard.)

Eldest girls are such a problem. What a king needs is a prince for his first born, not a princess. A nice clear line of succession makes for a nice stable realm. Besides, Dorothea was dead. You weren't going to thrive anyway.

(Sound of a baby crying.)

Harold thanked you, as his servant unwrapped your swaddling, for the sacrifice you were about to make to ensure the security of the realm. I considered calling up wild boars to take a run at him, big ones, preferably in search of companionship, but it's really not what I'm designed for. Fairy godmothers give gifts, and watch over their charges. So I watched as he left you on the ground, twelve hours old, naked and crying, ants already beginning to crawl over you. I watched as he rode back to look for a new mother for his son amidst his portraits of princesses—he'd had them brought out of storage before they cleaned up Dorothea's bloody bed clothes. I watched. *(Bending.)* Then I wrapped you in my cloak, *(She comforts the invisible child.)* and watched as you fell asleep on my useless old breasts. And then I took you to White Paws.

She'd just had her first litter. She sniffed you up and down, and then me, and for a moment I thought her interest might be culinary rather than maternal. She certainly looked like a big bad wolf. Then she rolled over, and offered you a teat. I laid you against her belly and you began to suck, and milk gushed into your starving little mouth and down your chin. I am not often ... happy. But I was then. Until I thought of Harold.

So I went to give Harold a gift. It's so hard, picking out just the right thing, but I finally hit on it, a nice case of the clap. When his new princess arrived, fifteen years old, and perfect, and saw his ulcerated skin and tremors, she could not, under threat of imprisonment, be brought to touch him. Nor did her papa insist, when it became painfully evident that the equipment Harold needed to consummate the marriage was due to drop off at any minute. *(She snorts.)* Poor Harold. *(Snort.)* May he rot in peace.

(MELISANDE chuckles into her gin. ROSE looks away.)

That made me feel a little better. *(She giggles.)* But not much. I have seen my princesses squandered on octogenarians, offered as door prizes at semi-annual invitational tourneys, sequestered, kidnapped, gilded, gelded and used as dragon bait. I thought I'd gotten sort of inured to the whole thing. But he threw you away like garbage. I decided that whatever he had, you were going to have. With the exception of the venereal disease, of course. You were going to inherit the kingdom. *(Pause.)* I was going to make sure of it.

It wasn't easy, you know. I'd never been a hands-on godmother before. Just show up at the christening and "I give her the gift of beauty," or grace, or pert breasts, or whatever the hell the mother had requested in the gift registry, then prang with the wand and my part was over. I didn't know anything about raising a child. And White Paws was no help at all. I mean she was a wonderful mother. Kept you clean and well-fed and savagely killed anything that tried to harm you. Exemplary. But I don't think she had the vaguest inclination regarding your future.

ROSE: Wolves don't think that way.

MELISANDE: What way?

ROSE: They don't think about the future. There's hungry and not. Tired and not. Alive—

MELISANDE: And not. Very philosophical.

ROSE: No. Wolves are not philosophical. They don't fret. They do what has to be done.

MELISANDE: And how is that determined?

ROSE: Wolf morals.

MELISANDE: Such as?

ROSE: Don't shit in the den.

MELISANDE: Words to live by.

ROSE: Stay with the pack. Kill quickly ... Protect the young.

MELISANDE: I tried, Rose.

ROSE: What?

MELISANDE: To protect you. Take care of you. I actually enjoyed it.

   (ROSE turns away.)

You were so ... new, and ... perfect. To look at you made me indulge in hope, for the first time in centuries.

   (Memory. ROSE is nine. She is playing at being a princess.)

ROSE: Am I pretty when I'm like this?

MELISANDE: You are pretty in almost any posture, including upside down with your tongue stuck out, as you will remember we discovered not long ago. Rose please, ladies do not squat.

ROSE: How do they pee, then?

MELISANDE: In private, and so it's anyone's guess in what position.

ROSE: I think they squat.

MELISANDE: Think what you like. Just don't do it in front of other people.

ROSE: My hair's getting longer.

MELISANDE: Hair will do that.

ROSE: If my hair was very long, would I look like a princess?

MELISANDE: As you are a princess, Rose, we can safely assume that you already look like a princess.

ROSE: Do not.

MELISANDE: I beg your pardon?

ROSE: I don't. Princesses are tall.

MELISANDE: Not when they're nine, they're not.

ROSE: Princesses have long, flowing tresses.

MELISANDE: And lice, in all likelihood.

ROSE: Princesses are delicate as rose petals, and soft-spoken as doves.

MELISANDE: Where are you getting this stuff?

ROSE: The books.

MELISANDE: Damn. What am I supposed to use to teach you to read? Maps? I thought I was safer with fairy tales than the Bible. Six of one, half a dozen of the other.

ROSE: I love fairy tales. Tell me the one about the princess on the glass mountain. And the handsome prince with the diamond ring and the golden horse.

MELISANDE: The princess had the diamond ring. And the horse was shod in gold.

ROSE: *(Cuddling against her.)* Once upon a time—

MELISANDE: Once upon a time there was a princess whose father placed her upon a mountain of glass with sides so slippery that no one could scale it. *(Looking down at ROSE.)* And after suffering a dreadful case of haemorrhoids from sitting on an ice cold skewer day and night, she died of starvation. The end.

ROSE: Do it right.

MELISANDE: What I'm going to do is get on with your lessons. So you can stop trying to divert me from that laudable plan of action, as I well know you're trying to do.

ROSE: I'm not at all like a princess, except that I'm pretty.

MELISANDE: You are your father's sole heir. Your father is a king. Therefore you are not only a princess, you are the crown princess, and eventual ruler of a snug, financially stable little kingdom with excellent potential for domestic growth. You are, therefore, a princess with a great deal to learn. Have you reviewed your history?

ROSE: If I do my lessons, will you tell me about the Lavender Princess and the Castle of Dreams?

MELISANDE: Good heavens, I knew her. A very sweet girl really. Wasn't her fault about the smell. Someone suggested to her parents that it would be a unique marketing ploy. They virtually pickled that child in a crock of lavender oil; she smelled wonderful, but she looked like a prune. And then, when the prince that finally got her turned out to be allergic—

ROSE: What was he like?

MELISANDE: Well enough, I suppose, except for the sneezing. It was his brother who was the real catch ... Prince Delbert D'or, or some such thing; part of him was made of gold, but for the life of me, I can't remember which part. It sounds uncomfortable, regardless ... you little wretch.

ROSE: What?

MELISANDE: Trying to avoid an education by playing on your dear old auntie's tentative hold on her faculties. History, Rose.

ROSE: C'mon Auntie Mel, once upon a time—

MELISANDE: After your lessons. If you dazzle me with your progress.

ROSE: It's so boring.

MELISANDE: No doubt. However, human beings are endlessly fascinated with tales of their own grotesquely mismanaged affairs. If you're going to fit in, you have to understand this twaddle.

ROSE: History. In such and such a date, one alpha male sprayed his scent all over such and such a place, then another sprayed over top. There was a lot of howling. Then the beta males all fought, 'til somebody showed somebody their belly. Then they all sniffed each other's tails, and mounted whatever bitches were still left. Then, in such and such a different date, they started spraying again.

MELISANDE: I really can't add much to that. Maybe we should move on to etiquette?

ROSE. We finished dessert spoons yesterday. I've got to go, Auntie Mel ... Mother's taking me hunting *(Smacking her lips.)* ... deer.

MELISANDE: I don't suppose you'll be using a dessert spoon—

ROSE: *(Demonstrating.)* Oh no ... first you break the neck, by biting right here ... then once it's down, you rip open the stomach lining, letting the lead male and female get the first blood *and* the liver—

MELISANDE: Rose, please—

ROSE: This is etiquette. Use the wrong spoon, and people just know you don't know which spoon to use; do the wrong thing at a kill and you lose an ear.

MELISANDE: My dear, at court, better to lose the ear.

ROSE: Why?

MELISANDE: To admit ignorance of aristocratic manners will cause you to lose status.

ROSE: Lower my tail.

MELISANDE: So to speak.

ROSE: *(Nodding.)* Less food ... weaker mate—

MELISANDE: In all likelihood.

ROSE: Show me about the spoons again.

MELISANDE: I'll make a queen of you yet. I'll take you back, and shove you right up Harold's nose.

ROSE: Yuck.

(MELISANDE swallows some gin.)

MELISANDE: I taught you everything I thought you needed to know: how to play a decent madrigal, row a light boat, fix an election. You'd read Pythagoras, Aquinas, Sappho, and the annotated journals of Lucretia Borgia, among other successful women. I gave you a vast if theoretical understanding of the world, and when your thirteenth birthday came, when you became a woman, what did you wish for, after all that training and enlightenment? A cure for the Black Plague? Peace in the Levantine? To save the unicorn?

(ROSE is now thirteen.)

ROSE: *(In a rush.)* I want my prince charming.

MELISANDE: What?

ROSE: I want to find my handsome prince, and fall in love with him, and him with me, and I want us to love each other forever.

MELISANDE: What about your kingdom?

ROSE: I don't want a kingdom, I want a prince.

MELISANDE: Rose, have you thought about this?

ROSE: I haven't thought about anything else.

MELISANDE: Rose, if you just need a fuck, I can bring someone in—

ROSE: It's not that. Why does everybody think it's that?

MELISANDE: Maybe it's the way you keep rubbing your thighs together.

ROSE: You. Mother. All the males in the pack, sniffing my bum, trying to get me to bend over. I don't want that. I want my handsome prince to sweep me up in his arms, and carry me off, and swear his undying love, and then—

MELISANDE: A good fuck.

ROSE: *(Fervently.)* Yah.

(MELISANDE steps out of the memory.)

MELISANDE: So you didn't want to inherit the kingdom. Fine. One thing I've gotten to be a true expert in is reduced expectations. Even if all you'd wanted was "happily ever after." A self-catering desert island, unlimited good books and a guide to greater joy through masturbation. Happiness is easy.

ROSE: *(Stepping out of the memory.)* I wanted love.

MELISANDE: You wanted "once upon a time."

ROSE: I wanted Charming.

MELISANDE: Well, you got him.

(MELISANDE watches as CHARMING gets up and joins ROSE in the memory, and the romantic struggle begins again.)

CHARMING: Hold still. Ow. You have no idea how close I came to shooting you.

(ROSE gives a snorting snarl.)

Damn. I mean, Charlie old son, don't mean to be critical, but seems you've just shot the woman of your dreams. Bit careless really. No, I'm afraid we don't have any replacement beautiful naked ladies, that was the only one in stock ... I couldn't believe it when you broke cover. Wow. She walks in beauty like the night—well, runs like hell, actually—and all that's best of dark and light meet in her aspect and in her eyes, *(Looking her up and down.)* and lots of other good places ...

(He pins her facing him.)

There be none of Beauty's daughters with a magic like thee.

(She knees him.)

Ouph. All right. So it isn't original. You'd be surprised how many women fall for it.

(He tackles her as she tries to run, turns her over to face him, under his body.)

Did I mention that you were beautiful? Yes. Bears mentioning again.

(He bends to kiss her. She gouges his cheek, and shimmies out from under him. He gets her foot, and she goes back down. Daubing the blood.)

I realize how much trouble I'm in here. I know how these things work. You go hunting and meet a beautiful nude woman running through the forest, she's probably a goddess or something. Get a goddess angry, and your chances of being turned into some embarrassing sort of animal are really quite good.

(ROSE roars with rage as he lifts her up.)

Though you seem to go for your basic maiming. Not the eyes please. The better to see you with, my dear. I'd love to know if you understand a thing I'm saying. I really think I'm going to have to mention the beautiful thing one more time. Easy ...

(He runs his hands down her back. She seems to relax, and as he begins to respond, she throws him.)

Shit!

(She breaks away.)

Don't leave.

(She stops, and looks back at him, staying carefully out of arm's reach.)

Oh please. Don't leave now. I've been looking for you all my life ... All my life ... All those women, who weren't you ... Diademia. Europa. Mimsy. God, they all blur together.

(He leans up, moving slowly, so not to startle ROSE.)

Mimsy was a lovely girl. Looked like an antelope ... big eyes, long legs ... blushed if you dangled a participle. She impaled herself on me my first night in her daddy's castle. You look dubious ... it's true, happens all the time ... Nab old Charlie if you can, that's what they all get told. He's not bad-looking, but if he had the face of wart hog you'd still jump him, and squeal like you were being brought off by an angel. 'Cause Charlie's so eligible it's indecent.

(ROSE is transfixed, and unaware that CHARMING has been slowly edging forward.)

Mirella, Angelicia, Windemara—if I'd met a plain Joan, I'd probably have married her. Is that your name? Joan?

(ROSE begins to answer. CHARMING does not notice.)

If Father had wanted the sort of fop who'd have taken one of those exquisite idiots to wife, he could have kept me at court after Mother died. He could have had me taught to minuet, and plot, and fuck boys just because I could get away with it. But he wanted a huntsman to succeed him. Good thing as it turns out. Or you might have—

(He lunges and grabs ROSE by the hair.)

—got away.

(The struggle played out in the opening scene takes place once again.)

What have you done?

ROSE: *(Lovingly.)* Bitten you at the carotid artery.

CHARMING: Why?

ROSE: So you'll bleed to death.

CHARMING: *(Kissing her again.)* Am I dying?

ROSE: No. *(Staring into his eyes.)* I didn't get a clean bite.

CHARMING: You can talk?

ROSE: *(Kissing him.)* Of course.

CHARMING: Who are you?

ROSE: *(Holding up a hand to be kissed.)* I am the Princess Rose.

CHARMING: Why didn't you speak, Princess Rose?

ROSE: We hadn't been properly introduced.

CHARMING: My name is Charming.

ROSE: Of course it is.

> *(She slides her arm through his, and they begin to stroll away.)*

CHARMING: Wait. You are real, aren't you?

ROSE: Compared to what?

CHARMING: My life up 'til now.

> *(She leans up, and he dodges. She gently bites him on the ear lobe, just enough to provoke an "ouch.")*

ROSE: See.

CHARMING: I love you.

ROSE: Of course you do.

> *(ROSE groans and leaves the memory, putting her head between her knees. CHARMING keeps moving.)*

MELISANDE: Nauseous?

ROSE: Uh.

MELISANDE: Me too.

ROSE: Huh?

MELISANDE: Yours is from being in your first trimester. Mine is from an overdose of treacle. I don't suppose you should be drinking, should you?

ROSE: *(Shaking her head.)* Protect the young.

CHARMING: Rose?

ROSE: Oh. *(Swallowing hard.)* Coming.

CHARMING: Rose, don't let Father frighten you.

ROSE: I won't.

CHARMING: Rose, stop it.

ROSE: What?

CHARMING: Rubbing.

ROSE: Why?

CHARMING: Rose, we did not make love on the horse.

ROSE: No.

CHARMING: Nor in the stable.

ROSE: No.

CHARMING: And Rose, a drowning man may want air more than I want you, but I doubt it.

ROSE: I can tell.

CHARMING: Everyone in a two mile radius will be able to tell if you don't stop doing that.

ROSE: But why?

CHARMING: I've been with hundreds of women, and I've had sneezes more memorable. I was looking for something ... I didn't know what ... actually, I'd given up looking. But then I saw your face, Rose. I saw you. And I knew you were what I was looking for. Now that I've found you, I am not going to screw you on the flagstones of the courtyard where everyone and his brother can watch.

ROSE: You aren't?

CHARMING: No. I'm going to marry you. And tell everyone and his brother to get their own girl.

ROSE: Okay.

(She presses against him.)

CHARMING: Yah ... *(Setting her at arm's length.)* Your Highness, if you would be kind enough to follow Lady Buttrell there, she will attire you.

(ROSE looks surprised.)

(Quietly.) I can do the princely if I have to ... *(Louder.)* His Royal Highness, my father, and I will attend you in the anteroom at your convenience.

(ROSE sweeps a careful curtsey to an unseen attendant, and exits.)

Look at her curtsey, in nothing but her hair. Look at Lady Buttrell, looking at her curtsey in nothing but her hair. *(Wincing.)* Down, big fella ... Oh. This is perfect. "Hello Dad. Had a bit of luck hunting. Caught a naked woman. Yes. Really. And—I'm going to marry her. Just one hitch. No one to give the lovely bride away. Hoped you'd stand in, Dad." I've often wondered what an apoplectic fit would look like.

(ROSE comes back, strapped into the dress. CHARMING steps back, and provides the voice of his father.)

CHARMING: *(As FATHER.)* What is your name?

ROSE: My name is Rose, and I am a princess.

CHARMING: *(As FATHER.)* Are you? And what is your portion, princess?

ROSE: I have none to speak of. I mean, I was brought up by a she-wolf named White Paws, and wolves aren't keen on property.

CHARMING: *(As FATHER, in a very loud stage whisper, outraged.)* Do you actually intend to marry this animal, without parents, land or dowry, regardless of your duty to the realm or me?

ROSE: My name is Rose, and I am a princess.

CHARMING: Of course you are. *(Stepping back in, loudly, for the benefit of eavesdroppers.)* If she can pass the test, Father, then she is a real princess, and I will marry her. If she does not ...

> *(He slips an arm around her, and gives her a private wink.)*

I will cast her out, and marry whoever you will.

> *(They watch him leave.)*

ROSE: I haven't had very much experience with humans, but I don't think it's healthy for his face to turn that colour.

CHARMING: We beat him, Rose.

ROSE: Did we?

CHARMING: Oh, yes. All you have to do is pass the test, and there isn't a damned thing he can do to stop us.

ROSE: What test?

CHARMING: The Princess Test. It's been the tradition here for generations.

ROSE: What do I have to do?

CHARMING: Sleep on a stack of twenty mattresses and twenty feather beds, with three peas under them all.

ROSE: That sounds easy enough.

CHARMING: If the peas bruise you, you pass.

ROSE: Charming. I've slept on the ground my whole life. On roots. Rocks.

CHARMING: You'll pass.

ROSE: Besides, what has a pea got to do with being a princess?

CHARMING: *(Sweeping her into his arms.)* It establishes your sublime delicacy.

ROSE: I haven't got one.

CHARMING: You'll pass.

> *(He begins to waltz her around.)*

ROSE: Charming? What if I'm not a real princess?

CHARMING: Shhh. Of course you're a real princess. You're my princess.

> *(He kisses her again and they dance. MELISANDE enters, and taps ROSE on the shoulder. She slips out of the dress, and CHARMING continues to dance with the dress.)*

ROSE: He was right ... I passed. I passed with flying colours. Black and blue, mostly. *(Steps up, limping a little.)* In the morning, Charming led me onto the balcony ...

> *(They play this out.)*

... and slipped the robe off my shoulders, oh so gently, and told me to turn around slowly, so they could see the bruises. And all the people cheered. And then ...

> *(They embrace and whirl around.)*

... we were married.

MELISANDE: And that was it? Just that once?

ROSE: Oh no. Every three months.

> *(ROSE watches as CHARMING sweeps up the dress and carries it off.)*

He was worth it. He was worth anything. We made love on my hair, in my hair, on the night we were married. Charming loved my hair. I lay down on it and Charming scattered roses all over me. Then he lay down and put his arms around me. I closed my eyes, and went inside this den of roses and legs and hair and kisses ...

> *(CHARMING is involved with the dress.)*

MELISANDE: *(To CHARMING.)* Stop that.

> *(He falls back.)*

Didn't it hurt?

ROSE: And the smell ... sweat and come and all those crushed roses—

MELISANDE: The thorns, Rose?

ROSE: And Charming ... Charming was everywhere, in me, on me, around me. All I could taste, all I could breathe, Charming and roses, charming and rose ... Charming in Rose ...

MELISANDE: The thorns, Rose, didn't they hurt?

ROSE: Of course they did.

> *(A wolf howl is heard.)*

MELISANDE: Of course they did. *(Pause.)* I heard it was a lovely wedding anyway. Pity White Paws couldn't attend.

ROSE: She wouldn't have been comfortable—

MELISANDE: You know that, do you?

ROSE: Charming said—

MELISANDE: Do tell.

ROSE: Charming said it was dangerous to let anyone know about my ... unusual upbringing.

MELISANDE: You were loved, Rose. Most human children can only dream of being loved the way White Paws loved you. In that, your upbringing was most unusual. Shocking, really.

ROSE: There were whispers, rumours. They said I wasn't really a woman, that I had Charming under an evil spell.

MELISANDE: I did warn you about the three-quarters of the human population which use their brains strictly as hat stands. Why did your mother have to suffer for their limitations?

ROSE: Charming had garlic shoved up his—

MELISANDE: Nose?

ROSE: No.

MELISANDE: Ouch.

ROSE: The cook put wolfsbane in my food. The archbishop pushed me into the moat and looked disappointed when I started to drown.

MELISANDE: You're an excellent swimmer.

ROSE: *(Pointing at the dress.)* Not in that thing I'm not.

MELISANDE: Right.

ROSE: You couldn't think of everything, Auntie Mel. There was always something more I didn't know. Something unusual.

> *(She sits at a remembered dinner table, with CHARMING beside her, making polite conversation to someone on his other side.)*

I didn't do anything stupid, Auntie Mel. I didn't growl or anything. Well. I thought about it. And maybe, if someone caught my eye when they were reaching for something I particularly wanted to eat—*(She follows an unseen reach and gives an intent look.)*—they'd decide to drop it.

> *(She watches the hand withdraw, smiles, and gracefully helps herself. CHARMING glances over, worried. MELISANDE looks stern and joins them at the table.)*

I wouldn't have bitten them. I just let them think I might. I got the cutlery right. And I drank my wine like a good human ...

> *(CHARMING pours her a glass. She lifts her glass and smiles.)*

... and I listened to them all fret. Fret about stuff that hadn't happened, and might not happen, but if it did happen, how fretful, and let's drink some more wine, so that we don't fret, we'll just get so stupid that we couldn't run if a bear was after us. *(She starts to weave sleepily.)* And all that food would just lay there, while they picked at it, and fretted. Maybe if you don't bring it down, you don't care as much about getting it inside of you.

(She climbs into CHARMING's lap, and starts to sleep on his shoulder. CHARMING is transfixed by embarrassment.)

MELISANDE: Rose. Rise and shine.

ROSE: I always sleep after a big meal. And they were all big meals.

MELISANDE: I'm sure this is going to lead somehow to an explanation of why you couldn't invite the creature that nursed and guarded you for your entire childhood to your wedding. But how is currently beyond me. The suspense is numbing.

ROSE: *(Opening an eye.)* Charming says the mother of the bride having fangs would put a damper on the festivities.

MELISANDE: Does he?

ROSE: *(Leaving the memory.)* You were invited, and you didn't come.

MELISANDE: Attend, when my dear friend White Paws wasn't invited? I couldn't have considered it.

ROSE: Just like that. You forget all about me.

MELISANDE: I didn't forget, Rose. You'd made your bed, however steep. As far as I could tell, you didn't want to do anything but lie on it. You got your wish. You got your prince and your castle of dreams. You didn't need me.

ROSE: I did too. I called and called. You never came.

MELISANDE: When?

ROSE: When? Night after night. Every time they attacked.

MELISANDE: Forgive me, dear, but, as is increasingly common, I don't know what you're talking about. Every time who attacked?

ROSE: The pack.

MELISANDE: White Paws' pack? Your family?

ROSE: Not any more.

MELISANDE: Is it not White Paws' pack any more, or is it not your family anymore?

ROSE: Both. Neither.

MELISANDE: Oh dear. Well, let's plunge in. I'm most comfortable in over my head. Why is it no longer your mother's pack?

ROSE: You should check your crystal ball more often, Auntie Mel. Mother died two years ago.

MELISANDE: Oh no … damn … I forget, you know. Time passes, and I think, is it an hour since I sat down? Is it a day? And then I look up, and it's years, and the children I've blessed are old women, with grandchildren drooling at their feet, and husbands drooling at their sides ... and wolves don't live as long as women. Damn. Were you with her?

ROSE: Not exactly.

MELISANDE: How do you attend your mother's deathbed inexactly?

ROSE: She was here.

MELISANDE: Here?

ROSE: They're always here. Day and night. Just one or two of my brothers, at first, outside the walls. Then packs of five or six, waiting to slip in whenever the gate opened. At it's worst there's been thirty, or forty, wolves I don't even know, from packs all over the country, raiding the castle almost every night. They made it to our bedchamber once, before the servants drove them out. And when they're not trying to get in, they're sitting, just out of bow reach, all around the castle, waiting for us. Waiting for me. And howling.

MELISANDE: How did your mother die?

ROSE: I was a lousy wolf. No fur, no fangs, a nose that's next to useless; I couldn't scent out a moose turd if it was dumped on my head. Did they think I could stay with them forever? There comes a point in a woman's life when eating raw voles and pissing on trees just isn't enough. I found my prince. I know I was very ungrateful to go off without saying goodbye, but there was Charming, and all that kissing ... and the next thing I knew I was taking the Test and then there was the wedding, and yes, White Paws should have come, but Charming ... doesn't understand about the pack ... I know I owe them everything, and I know they're angry, but I don't understand why they're doing this to me.

MELISANDE: How did White Paws die?

(CHARMING rises and stands behind ROSE, hands on her shoulders. ROSE's voice should come just after his.)

CHARMING: It was an accident.

ROSE: It was an accident.

MELISANDE: Shit.

ROSE: I'm sure she just wanted to get near him ... sniff him over ... I know Mother wouldn't ... hunt us.

ROSE and CHARMING: *(Together.)* One wolf looks much like another, to a human. There'd been so many attacks.

ROSE: Charming had been set upon constantly ... how was he to know she wasn't going to kill him—

CHARMING: Can you ever forgive me?

>   *(ROSE is bent over, grieving.)*

>   Rose? I'd cut off my hand if I could undo it. Please. Just say something.

>   *(Silence.)*

ROSE: Was it a good kill?

CHARMING: What?

ROSE: Quick. Clean.

CHARMING: Yes.

>   *(She curls against him, becoming as small as possible.)*

ROSE: Good. Good.

CHARMING: Is that all you have to say?

ROSE: What else is there to say?

MELISANDE: Absolutely nothing. Just kill him.

ROSE: It wasn't his fault.

MELISANDE: This *is* why you killed him ...?

ROSE: Accidents happen. Things die. Every wolf knows that. Mother knew that.

MELISANDE: She was my friend, Rose. I don't have many friends. Immortality seems to intimidate a lot of people. Not White Paws. She thought I smelled all right. We gift-givers don't get gifts very often, but your mother gave me her trust and regard, and I was honoured to receive it. Forgive me if I'm not as understanding as you about your prince hacking her to pieces.

ROSE: *(From CHARMING's arms.)* When he brought me her body, I felt like the marrow had been sucked from my bones. I couldn't think. I couldn't speak. I just lay on her, and howled for hours. And when I couldn't howl any more, I stopped. It was done. People carry on ... they're surprised when death doesn't make an exception for them ... wolves don't carry on. Wolves—

MELISANDE: Do what they have to do. I remember.

>   *(CHARMING sweeps her up in his arms, and carries her to the bed. Her eyes are closed and she's giggling.)*

ROSE: Why can't I look?

CHARMING: It's a surprise Rose. An ancient human custom.

ROSE: We were lifted in the air ... I felt that.

CHARMING: You peeked. Peekers are drawn and quartered you know. Another ancient human custom.

ROSE: I can always tell when you're lying. *(Sniffing his chest.)* You sweat when you're lying.

CHARMING: The sweat is from hauling you up here. *(Tossing her down.)* I was not lying, Rose, I was making a joke. The whole humour thing is taking a while, isn't it.

ROSE: I always laugh after you explain.

CHARMING: Commedias interruptus. It's just not the same.

ROSE: Where are we?

CHARMING: In the tower. This was my mother's room before her marriage to Father.

ROSE: Where's the door?

CHARMING: There is no door. We're forty feet above the highest room in the castle, and the only way out is through the window.

ROSE: This is one of those things that isn't going to make any sense, even when you do explain it, isn't it?

CHARMING: Probably. My mother stayed here until her wedding, with no access to the outside world, to guarantee her purity of mind and body.

ROSE: *(Sagely.)* Your father wanted to make sure the first litter was his.

CHARMING: My father doesn't leave things like that to chance, Rose. Mother was already carrying the first litter when she came up here, and you're looking at it.

ROSE: So first she proved she was fertile, then she proved that she hadn't been fertilized, only she had.

CHARMING: Uh huh.

(ROSE stares blankly for a moment.)

ROSE: Let's make love.

CHARMING: You always want to make love when you don't have a clue what I'm going on about.

ROSE: Is that a problem?

CHARMING: A problem? Rose, my Rose without thorns, it is the thing I like best about you—

ROSE: I thought my total animal passion in bed was the thing you liked best about me.

CHARMING: Oh, that too. God, yes. None of that "Couldn't we just talk," shit. No "I'm just not relaxed enough …" You just go at it, thwack.

(ROSE laps her chops and smiles.)

All teeth, and tongue, and noises.

(ROSE demonstrates.)

Sometimes I just lay there, wondering, is this the time she gobbles me up instead?

(ROSE chuckles, nibbles on his ear.)

And then you do gobble me up, so to speak, and I think, dear god, what a fool I am to be wasting my time thinking when my cock has just been struck by lightning. My brain is usually then swept by a wall of fire, there's smoke pouring out of every hole in my body, and then I generally convulse wildly and pass out—

ROSE: Is that unusual?

CHARMING: Rose, the Drinjaka bird of the Ebony Coast, who will nest only in the dung of pregnant elephants, and has the ability to survive being crushed under the feet of said pregnant elephants, by virtue of a skeleton made up entirely of cartilage, is unusual. You're a fucking freak of nature.

ROSE: That's good?

CHARMING: Rose ... that's perfect.

ROSE: Wait a minute.

CHARMING: Don't think I can.

ROSE: Why are we in the room with no door?

CHARMING: So no one can bother us.

ROSE: Good.

CHARMING: Stop. Rose.

ROSE: What?

CHARMING: Come here.

(He pulls her up, and wraps his arm around her.)

This is where you're going to stay.

ROSE: What?

CHARMING: They came too close, last night. Since ... the accident, we can't cross the courtyard safely, let alone go beyond the castle gates. I set guards. I stand guard myself, every night. They keep getting through.

ROSE: You want me to stay in this little room?

CHARMING: You've heard the gossip, Rose. They say the wolves are other men you've enchanted. They're always watching me. "Have you noticed all that body hair? Don't remember Charlie being quite so hirsute. And those fangs—wouldn't want to leave him alone with any small pets. Poor Charlie, he'll be scratching fleas and fetching balls for her before the winter's out." It just a matter of time until someone bashes your head in with a silver mace, or some such thing, to save me from your canine clutches. I can't keep you safe in the castle, and I can't keep you safe out. I don't know what else to do. It's just until I can sort out this whole problem with the wolves.

ROSE: I can't go out … at all?

CHARMING: I love you so much, Rose. Somebody should really warn people about this love stuff. I never realized what it would be like. The thought of losing you is … well, you know, you go into a fight, and you think, well I might die, but then again I might not, so I might as well get on with it. But losing you. I couldn't bear it. I've got to know you're safe. Safe and sound in the clouds. I've got to know you'll still be here when I come back. Just for a while. For me.

(They make love.)

MELISANDE: *(Interrupting.)* For him? You allowed yourself to be caged up so that Charming could have peace of mind? Think, Rose. Did you see a single silver mace? Were you actually hurt by any of the ravening wolves? Was anyone ever hurt except our hero here? Rose. Try to think with something above your belt for a second. Pant twice if you can hear me.

(She walks away in disgust.)

ROSE: You know what's the best thing about orgasms?

CHARMING: Surviving them?

ROSE: It's almost impossible to fret before, during or immediately after them.

CHARMING: Hmmm?

ROSE: See … there's the sharp part, right at first, and you can still sort of think, but all your thoughts are mostly, "oh boy here's the sharp part," and by the time it's spread down to your knees and toes and up through your teeth, you can almost manage an, "oh, I hope my leg doesn't cramp this time," but then it fills your brain … and there's no fretting, no thoughts at all—

CHARMING: Not even of me?

ROSE: Oh no. Nothing. That's the best part.

CHARMING: Is that why we do this three or four times a day?

ROSE: That, and for the exercise. I didn't think you minded.

CHARMING: Oh, well, it's hell of course. But for you, anything. But what are you fretting about?

ROSE: Nothing, when you're here. I'm just not used to being alone, you know, and I wonder, what happens if something goes wrong—

CHARMING: Like?

ROSE: Like ... my lungs stop working, or my heart just forgets to beat, while I'm sleeping, and I'm all alone and there's no one to notice that I'm dying—

CHARMING: That won't happen, if it did, I'd come and kiss my princess—

ROSE: —and I'd wake up and be alive again.

(CHARMING kisses her.)

CHARMING: *(Pulling away.)* I have to go. Do the princely.

(ROSE nods.)

Will you miss me?

ROSE: Yes.

CHARMING: Do you love me?

ROSE: Yes.

CHARMING: And I love you.

ROSE: Of course you do.

(The memory begins to slip away. CHARMING is somehow absent, either prone, or withdrawn, or out of the light.)

We fell into a nice little routine, in our nice little room, just me and Charming in here, and the wolves out there, and every three months or so, just to prove to everyone outside of the tower that I continued to be a real princess ... I took the test.

(She leans against the bed, wincing, almost falls, CHARMING catches her in a sweep of his arms, and kisses her on her arms and back, she flinches with each kiss; each is a bruise. He carries her to the window. She is crying as she goes through the display ritual. He rocks her, humming as she presses against his shoulder. She dries her face against him, and nestles there. Defiantly.)

All in all, it was a very happy marriage.

(CHARMING carries her back to the bed, and strokes her hair, she seems to fall asleep.)

CHARMING: *(Touching her bruises.)* Look. There's one on her face. Poor Rosie. Does it hurt? Of course it hurts, stupid. It's a bruise. Sorry, Rose. If only I'd never seen your face. If only you'd run a little faster. If I'd never seen your face, I'd never have known that I couldn't live without seeing your face, and so, I could have. You follow me so far, sweetie? Of course, you don't.

I saw this gorgeous face yesterday. Came with big breasts, narrow waist, the kind of ass that offers a broad but firm handhold. Gave me this silk sheets/ostrich feathers/lots of honey look. Type C, the full bodied exotic fuck, always a favourite of mine. Nothing. Not a twitch. A hump-backed eighty-five year old nun could not have stirred me less. And I thought monogamy was going to be difficult. Because I thought it had something to do with free will. But that was before Rose's face got me.

I don't know why I'm complaining. At the rate we go at it, who needs variety? It's just that ... I'm not sure about this being got. Once in a while I'd like to get her. I'd like to get far enough inside of her to reach whatever it is that's got me and get it back. Get some rest. But just when I think I'm gonna make it, when I think all I have to do is hold out one more minute and I'll have her for a change, it dawns on me that I'm not going to make it; I'm not going to be able to hold out a whole minute, because a minute is the longest stretch of time conceivable. Because I would sooner be rubbed with pork fat and thrown naked to starving jackals than hold out one more second. And then I give it all away, my self-control, my self-respect, my self entirely. She takes it all. She takes me. And all I can think about doing is trying to get her, again.

And I don't even know what I'm trying to get. See, Rose may be part wolf, but she's all woman. And women are ... different. A completely different form of life. I don't think God created women. I think they were sitting around, well before the first light, talking, yack-a-yack-a-yack, figuring it all out. How they were going to handle men. How they were going to get us.

And then when God let there be light, he looked down, and there was his planet, thick with these beautiful, mysterious creatures, looking smug. What was he supposed to do? The first man was already staggering out of the mud. He'd already seen them. His prick was about to lead him where God would fear to tread. He'd been got. I suspect God invented free will at that moment, so he could wash his hands of the whole, doomed mess.

And the women? They looked at that poor, unsuspecting bastard, with his hard-on aimed like a divining rod for disaster, and looked at each other, and laughed themselves silly.

It's all in the genitals. The penis is an upright, forthright, straightforward organ. You know where you stand with a penis. But the clitoris? How long do you suppose it took them to come up with that one? "So you have this big dangling thing that sits up and begs like a schnauzer, do you? Well we have this tiny little bump, that's never in the same place twice, and we want you to go hunting through the underbrush for it whilst dazed with lust, and if you don't find it, you can tell your schnauzer to lie down, cause walkies is over." Jesus.

(MELISANDE has been listening, and now moves to the edge of the bed.)

MELISANDE: You're not asleep Rose. And ladies do not eavesdrop.

ROSE: Ladies do if they want to have the vaguest idea what gentlemen really think. Quiet. This is the best part.

CHARMING: Of course, the migratory clitoris isn't a problem with Rose. Hers doesn't wander. It spreads. Gets to the point where she comes when I rub her thumbs ... If I ever took her to a party, I be cuckolded fifteen times before she got to the punch bowl, based on handshakes alone. Never mind dancing. Tread on her toes while dancing and she'd howl with unspeakable delight ...

Wonder how Father likes listening to that every night. Bet he lies there, holding his breath and his stubby old dick, waiting for the howl. I hope so. I hope he lays there, pronging his pillow, calling it Rose and hating me. Whenever I feel I can't rise to Rose's occasion, I think of that. Works like a charm.

He can't stand that I've finally got something that he didn't give me. Something he can't take away. You're mine. You may not be house-broken. You may not get my jokes. But you've got me, Rosie. And so, the only way to get myself back, is to have you. And I do, don't I sweetie? I do have you.

ROSE: He loves me. He really does. *(Pause.)* He had to do it.

MELISANDE: He had to do what, Rose? What?

ROSE: *(Whisper.)* Help me pass the Test.

(She puts on the dress, and goes to stand beside him. He slips his arm around her shoulder.)

MELISANDE: *(Between them.)* You knew?

ROSE: Not at first. But ... I don't like wine. I was supposed to drink wine from this very fancy cup, before I took the Test, even after we moved. But I just hate going to sleep without knowing that I can wake up, if I have to, so, so, one night I just didn't drink it, and—

MELISANDE: And that's when you found out the wine was drugged. Because you woke up. Because you could wake up, for the first time, and you did have to.

(ROSE lies on the bed. Lights dim. CHARMING crosses, and stands, a little unsteadily. He has a riding crop.)

ROSE: I could smell wine on him. A lot. Charming has to drink a lot before it affects him. And he was quite affected.

CHARMING: Ssssh. Charlie's got to do it, Rosie. Got to do the princely. Dear old Dad says. Dear old Dad must be obeyed.

(He hits her. She opens her eyes.)

MELISANDE: Rose, come out of there immediately.

(She lies still, looking up at him. He hits her again.)

Rose.

(ROSE leaves the dress behind.)

So you opened your eyes, and saw him.

(CHARMING hits the dress.)

Well. Isn't this where you kill him?

(ROSE just stares, flinching with each hit.)

CHARMING: What's a few bruises, says Dad. She could have got them tripping over her skirts. And everyone goes baaa *(Hit.)* baaa *(Hit.)* baaa *(Hit.)* poor old Charlie's been had. *(Hit.)* She's got Charlie by the short and curlies. Wolf whipped. Makes him sit up and beg. Dad just sits on his bony old ass, *(Hit.)* waiting for me to give it up, and be a good little prince. Thinks he's got me. Bastard. I know how Mother passed the Test.

MELISANDE: You opened your eyes Rose, and then what did you do?

ROSE: I closed them.

CHARMING: There. *(Hit.)* There. *(Hit.)* You won't go away now. He can't make you go away. Not this time.

(He lies down beside the dress, and draws it to him, and passes out. ROSE bends over him.)

MELISANDE: You closed them?

ROSE: He was doing it for me. I'm no princess. I could no more feel those peas than I could fly. He knew. He saved me. My prince rode up the glass mountain, and saved me. Because he loved me.

MELISANDE: You know, I've seen love. I've also seen meat tenderized. That really looked more like the latter.

ROSE: You don't understand.

MELISANDE: Oh, that's where your wrong, chick. You think you're the first of my girls to be loved so intensely? He was beating the shit out of you with a riding crop. I don't know, Rose. It may seem odd to you, but some people would find that annoying—

ROSE: It was my fault. I wished for him. And I didn't deserve him. Somewhere there's a real princess, one who's beautiful, and delicate and pure and all those things Charming thinks I am; someone who could pass the Test. And she's dying a little bit every day, because Charming doesn't come. Because I've got him. I think about her, all alone and sad, and aching for him, and I don't care what I have to do to keep him. I'm a lousy princess, and I'm a lousy wolf, but Charming loves me. That's who I am, I'm Charming's Rose. That's all I am.

MELISANDE: *(Pause.)* Well dear, I thought I understood this ... but obviously I'm completely off the mark. Rose, what happened to Charming?

ROSE: I got pregnant.

MELISANDE: I know. But Rose, nausea, water retention, sure ... but this? *(She gestures to CHARMING.)*

ROSE: Charming ...

> *(She goes and sits in the window. CHARMING joins her, and they sit quietly. He rubs her back. Pause. They listen to the howling.)*

CHARMING: Do you know, I can't sleep the nights they don't come.

ROSE: Just a few tonight.

CHARMING : What are they saying?

ROSE: Wolves don't say. They sing.

CHARMING: What are they singing?

ROSE: Lots of things. Come here. Threat. Wait.

CHARMING: Wait for who?

ROSE: Not for who. For what.

CHARMING: All right, my interlocutor, wait for what?

ROSE: Killing. Wait for killing.

CHARMING: A soothing lullaby ... shouldn't you be asleep?

ROSE: *(Speaking on "shouldn't you.")* About the Test.

CHARMING: What about it?

ROSE: Well, it's been getting ... harder ... there were the broken ribs last time.

CHARMING: It was the talk of the court. They want that particular set of peas for the state museum.

MELISANDE: *(In a stage whisper.)* You didn't tell him that you knew?

ROSE: *(Without turning.)* Oh no. He couldn't bear that. *(To CHARMING.)* I can't take the Test while I'm pregnant.

CHARMING: Pregnant?

ROSE: Well, Charming, we have sex all the time. People get pregnant from that, you know.

CHARMING: I had wondered about that. Thank you for clearing it up.

ROSE: You're welcome. I know which time it was. I'll bet you don't even remember. It was right after you came back from that long hunting trip, remember. I missed you so much, and you were so tired, and we just fell asleep. Just the smell of you was enough. Then I woke up a little later, and it was so dark. Remember? There was no moon. I couldn't see your face, I couldn't see my hands, but I could feel yours. All over me. I thought I was dreaming. I'd been having dreams like that, every night you were away. But I wasn't. When you pulled away, I knew you weren't all gone. There was something in there. Something new. I could feel it, glowing. Filling up all my empty spaces.

CHARMING: That's why you think you're pregnant?

ROSE: I know how to tell. Want to feel my cervix?

CHARMING: No.

ROSE: I know. I'm carrying your baby. So I can't take the test.

CHARMING: I'm afraid you have to, Rose.

ROSE: I could lose the baby.

CHARMING: Yes.

ROSE: Lose the baby. Our baby.

CHARMING: *(Rubbing her back again.)* Having a baby is dangerous, Rose. There's no need for you to go through it. Don't feel you have to carry on the family line. It's undoubtedly the only thing you could do that would please Father, and we wouldn't want that. *(Pause.)* Rose? Is it so unbearable being just you and me? Alone? In our bed in the sky. You're everything to me. Aren't I everything to you?

ROSE: I can't take the test.

CHARMING: They say that sometimes princesses change during a confinement. *(He looks at her.)* A confinement, Rose. A pregnancy.

ROSE: I know—

CHARMING: That they can lose whatever it is that makes them real.

(Pause.)

ROSE: I'll go ... somewhere. Until the baby—

CHARMING: Where? Do you know a place where the wolves can't find you? The only place I know is here, behind the walls, with men and spears and torches. And Father ... Think, Rose. There's nowhere to go but here. And Father will throw you out of here, to the wolves if you refuse the Test. You'll lose the baby anyway. And I'll lose you. I'd die if I lost you. Is that what you want?

ROSE: Charming. Please.

CHARMING: I wish this didn't have to be. I wish the world was perfect. It's close, Rose. It's so close, when I'm with you.

ROSE: There must be another way.

CHARMING: I'd tell you if there were.

ROSE: There's no other way?

CHARMING: Do you have to ask?

ROSE: Yes. You know me. I have to have things explained.

CHARMING: There's no other way.

> *(Pause.)*

ROSE: I have to do it, then.

CHARMING: That's my brave princess.

ROSE: Brave. Yes. I can be that. *(Pause.)* Let's make love. Slowly.

CHARMING: Yes, your majesty.

ROSE: Slowly.

CHARMING: Rose.

ROSE: Slower … slower … *(Draping her hair around them, as if self-conscious for the first time.)* You've got me, Charming. You've got all of me … This is all of me …

> *(After a passionate embrace, ROSE slides down his body, and at the moment when it cannot happen, breaks his neck. When he dies, ROSE throws her head back and both howls and screams over the body. Silence. As MELISANDE approaches, ROSE grips CHARMING to her and snarls, MELISANDE jumps back. Silence.)*

MELISANDE: Kill quickly.

> *(ROSE looks up.)*

Protect the young.

> *(ROSE seems to see MELISANDE again, nods a little.)*

The very young.

> *(ROSE starts to shake.)*

Sweetheart? Rosebud? *(She puts her arms around ROSE.)* It's going to be all right. *(Stroking her hair.)* … Wolves are not philosophical, are they, Rose? They do what has to be done … You couldn't let him kill the baby, could you? And you couldn't leave. So you did what had to be done. For what it's worth, White Paws would have been very proud of you.

> *(ROSE stares.)*

It was a magnificent kill. Clean, fast and ... *(Looking at CHARMING.)* necessary. She couldn't have done better herself. And she did try.

ROSE: *(Trying to pull away.)* Charming?

MELISANDE: Let him rest a little. *(Looking at CHARMING.)* Poor boy. So handsome. So ... damaged.

ROSE: It's not supposed to end like this.

MELISANDE: No. No Rose, it's supposed to end like this.

> *(CHARMING stands, brings the dress to the bed, and stands over it.)*

And in the end, there was a princess, white as snow, lying on her sheets, red as blood, and her prince, in mourning black as ebony, stood beside her.

> *(CHARMING kisses where ROSE's face would be were she wearing the dress, and waits. Nothing happens.)*

CHARMING: You said you'd wake up ... *(Stands up, wiping his eyes.)* I have to go ... do the princely.

> *(ROSE nods.)*

ROSE: *(To MELISANDE.)* Why couldn't I die for him?

MELISANDE: Rose. I made many mistakes. Dorothea gave you her beauty. White Paws gave you her strength. And if I'd been content with being your auntie, I would have given you joy, which is always a nice gift, and ugly sweaters on your birthday. But I wanted to be your mother too. I wanted to give you what I had. What I had was rage. So I wrapped my rage in nice manners and pretty clothes and dancing feet, and tried to give it to you. And all the while I was thinking how clever I was, because I was going to send my rage out into the world, disguised as a princess. And before anyone could figure out that under all that satin and hair was my rage, under it all was a wolf in princess's clothing, you would have taken back everything that had been stolen from you, from me, from all my girls. And eased my rage. I wasn't thinking of you. I was thinking of me. That was a mistake.

I just assumed you'd know which was the gift and which was the wrapping. Mistake number two. When you threw away my rage, and kept all that princess crap, I made the worst mistake. I gave up on you. But there is one mistake I did not make. I did not teach you to die for love.

ROSE: He said he'd die for me.

MELISANDE: He's a man of his word.

CHARMING: *(To the dress.)* Will you miss me?

ROSE: Yes.

   (He can't hear her.)

CHARMING: Do you love me?

ROSE: Yes.

CHARMING: Well, do you?

ROSE: Yes.

CHARMING: I love you.

MELISANDE: Things don't actually end, Rose. That's the fairy tale. Once upon a time, things happened, and once they'd happened, they were gone, and the future stretched ahead without a whiff of the shit that had hit the past lingering. It's a male view of time. Comes of not scrubbing enough toilets. So Rose, in the absence of an ending, I'll give you a beginning. Once upon a time, there was Rose in a warm room with a dead man, and a beautiful baby boy in her belly. There were wolves, but not ravening ones; just tired, and hoarse, and very anxious to have her back. There was space, and sky, and falling to sleep without dreading what she'd wake to. And there was her foolish old aunt, who looked at her, and continued to indulge in hope. Tell me what comes next, Rose. Tell me what you wish.

   (Music up. Lights down. The end.)

I Hate You
on Mondays

by
Kate Miles

I Hate You on Mondays was originally presented in an independent production at the Theatre Passe Muraille Backspace from November 22 to December 3, 1995, with the following cast:

BERNADETTE	Christine Brubaker
MOTH	Shawn Pitch
PINCH	Derek Metz

Directed by Jennifer Brewin
Set Design by Wendy Robbins
Lighting Design by Jaime Farley
Stage Manager: Joann Roberts
Assistant Satge Manager: David Anderson
Production Manager: Debbie Read
Sound Consultant: Scott White
Photography: D. Geoffrey Hyde

*to the students and staff
of SEED Alternative School,
past, present, and future*

Characters

BERNADETTE: Female, nineteen years old.
MOTH: Male, fifteen years old.
PINCH: Male, twenty-one years old.

Setting

The play takes place in present-day
downtown Toronto, over four weeks in spring.

Scene One

(Night. BERNADETTE and PINCH burst into his basement apartment, all over each other. PINCH falls on the army cot, taking BERNADETTE with him. They struggle to untie his boots. Lights out. Night. BERNADETTE sits up gasping.)

Scene Two

(Morning. BERNADETTE maneuvers her way out from under PINCH's arm and starts retrieving her clothes from the floor. PINCH wakes up, goes into an immediate coughing fit, then pulls a dusty six-pack out from under the bed and opens a beer.)

PINCH: Jesus fuck!

(He sees a cockroach on the floor and stomps on it.)

I hate bugs. My brother used to tell me that earwigs would go in your ears—

BERNADETTE: And infest your brain.

PINCH: Kids told that to you, too?

BERNADETTE: No, I told it to other kids.

PINCH: And I'd have nightmares where I'd try to talk and earwigs would crawl out of my mouth and walk all over my face and eat my eyes. Want a beer?

BERNADETTE: I gotta split.

PINCH: You're leaving?

BERNADETTE: I have to go to church.

PINCH: Excuse me?

BERNADETTE: Big building. God's place.

PINCH: Right … This is going to sound awful, but I don't remember your name.

BERNADETTE: Oh, it's cool. Bernadette.

PINCH: You're Catholic?

BERNADETTE: No, United.

PINCH: Understandable.

BERNADETTE: Have you got a token?

PINCH: Like I still go to confession when I remember and stuff, but I can't see why any woman would want to be Catholic.

BERNADETTE: *(Laughing.)* Please don't.

PINCH: Don't what?

BERNADETTE: Please don't use women's rights as a come-on line. Next thing you'll be wanting to walk me around the block so you can tell me why you think date rape is like, really bad.

PINCH: Why would I need to hit on you?

BERNADETTE: Beats me. We already had sex.

PINCH: I'm just trying to make conversation.

BERNADETTE: I'm taking your token. Morning service starts at eleven.

PINCH: You really have to go?

BERNADETTE: *(Wide-eyed.)* Well, gosh, um—

PINCH: Pinch.

BERNADETTE: Well, gosh, Pinch, I'd love to stick around and whip up a bunch of pancakes for you and the rest of the atonal delinquent gang, that would be just swell, but they need me in the choir.

PINCH: You're full of shit.

BERNADETTE: No, I'm serious, man, it's a mess. Six altos got mono playing Spin the Bottle during Christian Youth.

(PINCH kisses her.)

Whoa ... hold still.

(She smacks him.)

Bug.

PINCH: Thanks.

BERNADETTE: You really go to confession?

PINCH: Every couple of weeks, yeah. Got to make sure I'm squeaky clean in case I get hit by a bus.

BERNADETTE: Fuck. I just wear clean underwear. Bye.

Scene Three

(Afternoon. BERNADETTE is dyeing MOTH's hair.)

MOTH: Ow! Fuck off, 'Dette, you're getting it in my eyes.

BERNADETTE: Grab a towel.

MOTH: I can't see! Ow!

BERNADETTE: It's to your left.

> *(MOTH reaches to the right.)*

Left, Moth, left.

MOTH: Okay. Go on.

BERNADETTE: So we get to his place, it's this basement hole, the whole band's there—

MOTH: Did you meet them?

BERNADETTE: No, we went straight to his room. And it's full of sound equipment and dirty shirts and we go at it on this green army cot. And then I understand what he's saying.

MOTH: What?

BERNDETTE: It's "Hail Mary full of grace the Lord is—"

MOTH: Fuck off.

BERNADETTE: I swear to … me. And outside his bedroom the drummer and the bass player are beating each other up and I can hear the drummer's skull bashing against the wall and the bass player's yelling, "I'm going to fucking kill you," over and over so every time he goes, "Pray for us sinners now and at the hour of our death," I swear he's talking about me 'cause I'm convinced that the drummer's head is going to bash right through the wall any second and I'm going to die.

MOTH: Did you leave?

BERNADETTE: After? Yeah. I stole a token and told him I had to go to church.

MOTH: You make no sense.

BERNADETTE: It's the only plausible excuse to leave on a Sunday morning.

MOTH: Yeah, and they think you're so fucked up they never want to see you again.

BERNADETTE: Tell me about it. It was fucking dismal, they've put up this huge felt banner with "Jesus Loves You" spelled out in macaroni.

MOTH: You actually went? Again?

BERNADETTE: Well, I don't like to lie. My mom was thrilled. Here, roll.

> *(She tosses a dope tin at him.)*

MOTH: What happened to your mouth?

BERNADETTE: His boot. He stagedived into this patch of anorexic school-for-the-arts girls and they just collapsed.

(Beat.)

So what did you do last night?

MOTH: I played Yahtzee with my brother.

(*BERNADETTE gets up and starts fiddling with his shower cap.*)

BERNADETTE: It'll get better when you start growing facial hair.

MOTH: Bernadette.

BERNADETTE: Yes, my child.

MOTH: What colour is my hair?

BERNADETTE: Blue.

MOTH: *Blue?*

BERNADETTE: Yep.

MOTH: Like a blue-black.

BERNADETTE: No, like a Smurf.

MOTH: You dyed my hair blue.

BERNADETTE: I had, like, a vision. I was picking up my pills and it just hit me: Moth must have blue hair. Then he will get laid.

MOTH: Fuck off … Hoover.

BERNADETTE: What did you call me?

MOTH: Hoover.

BERNADETTE: Where'd you hear that?

MOTH: School.

BERNADETTE: I knew this would be a problem.

MOTH: What?

BERNADETTE: Us going to the same school.

MOTH: It's not my fucking fault. You were supposed to be gone.

BERNADETTE: I'm grazing.

MOTH: You're flunking.

BERNADETTE: Bite me.

MOTH: Why do they call you Hoover?

BERNADETTE: Because I like to clean.

MOTH: Okay.

(*She notices blue dye on her shirt and takes it off.*)

No, it's not.

BERNADETTE: Very good. Because I gave thirteen blow jobs at a CNE concert when I was fourteen.

(Beat.)

MOTH: Were there thirteen guys?

BERNADETTE: No, there were twelve.

MOTH: Why?

BERNADETTE: It was a bet with my friends for the price of my ticket.

MOTH: Oh my god.

BERNADETTE: Don't look at me like that. It was funny. I was blasted on an inch of booze from every bottle in my mom's liquor cabinet. *Funny*, Moth. Ha ha ha.

MOTH: Ha. Wait a second, when you were fourteen?

BERNADETTE: Yeah.

MOTH: When you were my babysitter?

BERNADETTE: Yeah.

MOTH: You would suck off double-digit numbers of guys and then come over and help me brush my teeth?

BERNADETTE: I was a great babysitter.

MOTH: You forgot to feed us.

BERNADETTE: Once.

MOTH: Twice.

BERNADETTE: There was a famine in Ethiopia. You needed to be aware.

(Beat.)

Moth?

MOTH: Dye it back.

BERNADETTE: Too late.

MOTH: Bullshit.

BERNADETTE: You said you were bored.

MOTH: My dad's gonna freak.

BERNADETTE: It's *your* head.

MOTH: Just because your mom is really cool—

BERNADETTE: She's not cool, she just works nights.

MOTH: Whatever.

BERNADETTE: You're fifteen. It's a universal excuse. Use it.

MOTH: I hate you on Mondays. You're always in this punchy mood and you hum those awful songs from church.

BERNADETTE: I do not.

MOTH: You've been humming "Tell Me the Stories of Jesus" for the past hour.

BERNADETTE: Oh shit, it's invading my brain.

MOTH: Yeah, with catchy tunes.

BERNADETTE: As opposed to?

MOTH: I dunno, a moral code?

BERNADETTE: You know what I think you should be when you grow up? A Puritan. We've got like a shortage. There's a gap in the market.

MOTH: We have our family portrait next week. My parents are going to implode.

BERNADETTE: Tell them it was me. Tell them I forced you into it.

MOTH: You did.

BERNADETTE: They used to pay me to take care of you—

MOTH: That's not going to help me, 'Dette. They haven't forgotten that time.

BERNADETTE: What time?

MOTH: You know.

BERNADETTE: No.

MOTH: When you took off to that boozecan and I had to take care of Tyler—

BERNADETTE: Ohh shit, am I going to have to pay for this in blood—

MOTH: And I dropped him.

BERNADETTE: Fine.

MOTH: On his head.

BERNADETTE: He was okay—

MOTH: He got a concussion.

> *(BERNADETTE lights the joint MOTH has rolled and refuses to speak.)*

> 'Dette? Look, all I'm saying is, they're not going to forgive me just because … Bernadette? God, would you put a shirt on please?

> *(BERNADETTE puts on a shirt.)*

BERNADETTE: *You* dropped him.

MOTH: Fine. I dropped him.

BERNADETTE: Okay.

> *(BERNADETTE starts taking off the shower cap and towelling his head.)*

MOTH: I was nine years old, but—

BERNADETTE: Shut. Up. Change the subject.

(Beat.)

MOTH: Okay. How did you lose your virginity?

BERNADETTE: My what?

MOTH: Virginity!

BERNADETTE: *How* did I lose it? I bust up my hymen.

MOTH: Gross!

BERNADETTE: You're done.

MOTH: How does it look?

BERNADETTE: What's the worst they can do, ground you? So you'll spend all your time in your room, what else is new?

MOTH: No. They'll make me volunteer at my uncle's bingo hall.

BERNADETTE: Cool.

MOTH: No, not cool. Have you ever been to a bingo hall, Bernadette? It's like this big smoky sea of velour with hot dogs. It's fucking grim.

BERNADETTE: Cool.

MOTH: It's not funny. Bingo is hell.

(BERNADETTE holds up a mirror. Beat.)

Did you ever consider the possibility you might be truly evil?

BERNADETTE: Um ... no.

Scene Four

(Night. PINCH kneels at the confessional.)

PINCH: Bless me father for I have sinned. It has been three weeks since my last confession. These are my sins. Okay. I have ... taken drugs, smoked on the subway, had premarital sex, stolen bikes, and taken the Lord's name in vain. I forgot to feed my cat and it died. I broke Rick's collarbone because he broke the neck of my guitar. And my dad called the bar to ask me to come back to New Liskeard, and I—I told him to shove it.

(Beat.)

And for these I am truly, truly sorry. I know it doesn't look like it but I'm still struggling, I swear. But it's like wrestling with demons made of Jello, man, it's too fucking—sorry. You know, I think I'd do better if being a celibate, drug-free, law-abiding good son was somehow ... appealing.

(Beat.)

But then it wouldn't be a struggle, yes, I understand.

Scene Five

(Afternoon. MOTH and BERNADETTE are drunk on the street, passing a bottle back and forth and people-watching.)

MOTH: What about that guy?

BERNADETTE: Which one?

MOTH: Bleached hair.

BERNADETTE: God no. He looks like a Q-tip.

MOTH: And him?

BERNADETTE: What do you think?

MOTH: Fixation with pornography.

BERNADETTE: Very good.

MOTH: What about him?

BERNADETTE: Small dick.

(Beat. MOTH looks horrified.)

I'm kidding, baby, I can't tell.

MOTH: Don't call me baby. Hey, there's one for you.

(He points to PINCH, busy postering.)

BERNADETTE: Shit. That's BVM boy.

MOTH: You want me to leave, don't you?

(BERNADETTE kisses him on the forehead.)

Get off me!

BERNADETTE: Thanks.

(MOTH exits. BERNADETTE walks towards PINCH.)

Hey.

PINCH: It's the AWOL babe.

BERNADETTE: Excuse me?

PINCH: AWOL. Absent With Out Leave.

BERNADETTE: I told you, I had to go to church.

PINCH: You didn't want to have breakfast with me.

BERNADETTE: *No*, I'm sure it would have been great—

PINCH: It could have—

BERNADETTE: Yeah, we could have gone to the Vesta and tried to digest some eggs, exchanged hangover remedies—You could have asked me awkward questions like, "So ... do you have any brothers or sisters?" "Did you grow up in Toronto?" "Are you a vegetarian?" And then I would write my name on the inside of your cigarette pack and you'd never phone me.

PINCH: Shit.

BERNADETTE: I really do go to church.

(PINCH continues postering.)

PINCH: Hold down these corners.

BERNADETTE: These?

PINCH: Yeah.

(Beat.)

Do you like stew?

BERNADETTE: Why?

PINCH: I make stew. My mom taught me. It tastes different every time.

(BERNADETTE is visibly wincing.)

BERNADETTE: Is this a—

PINCH: Not! It's a ... thing. Why, do you have a—

BERNADETTE: Ha ha! No.

PINCH: I wanted you to stay. You don't do the neck thing.

BERNADETTE: Excuse me?

PINCH: The neck thing. The other girls, they're always giggling and putting their hand on my arm and doing this thing with their neck.

(He cocks his head to one side.)

Pisses me off. I'm always thinking they'll end up paralyzed or something and it'll all be my fault. Plus, you're cute.

(BERNADETTE punches him in the solar plexus.)

Ow!

BERNADETTE: Don't call me cute.

PINCH: Okay.

BERNADETTE: Would you like to sit down?

PINCH: Thanks.

BERNADETTE: Sorry. It's a reflex.

PINCH: Understandable.

BERNADETTE: So ... okay.

PINCH: Cool. Plus, we already had sex.

BERNADETTE: This is true.

(Lights shift to MOTH in his bedroom.)

Scene Six

(Night. BERNADETTE sits up in bed, gasping. PINCH sits up beside her. She puts her hand over his face and pushes him back down.

A phone rings. Lights shift to MOTH answering his phone.)

MOTH: It's the middle of the night. *(Pause.)* Ohh shit, okay, breathe, all right? *(Pause.)* Meet me at the bench.

(Lights shift to BERNADETTE on a park bench, covered in sweat. She takes out a safety pin and begins methodically pricking her bare knee. MOTH comes up behind her.)

MOTH: Holy shit. You're drenched.

BERNADETTE: You think I don't know that? What time is it?

MOTH: Three forty-seven.

BERNADETTE: Fuck. Sit down.

MOTH: Thanks, Moth. Oh, no problem, my pleasure. Do you mind? No, no, I think sleep is overrated. I think I have like a dependency on rest, I'm trying to work past it.

BERNADETTE: Shut up.

(MOTH reaches over and snatches the pin away.)

MOTH: You're the only woman I know who's convinced she's secretly a blow-up doll.

BERNADETTE: Leave me alone. I'm praying. My God's growing a beard.

MOTH: I thought you said God was the balance that made beautiful people stupid.

BERNADETTE: None of that earthy shit works if you think you're going to die. It sucks, every six months I'm forced to bargain with this temperamental, like—

MOTH: Cecil B. DeMille God.

BERNADETTE: Yeah, and the fucking patriarchal bastard's crying huge rainstorms for starving telethon kids and sluts like me. Asshole.

MOTH: I can't believe you're only religious when it's convenient.

BERNADETTE: Duhh, moron. That's kind of the tradition.

MOTH: I don't fucking know these things. My family goes to Golden Griddle on Sundays.

BERNADETTE: Oh, your family's got their own religion.

MOTH: Yeah, what?

BERNADETTE: Some weird fucking "We cheer really loud at sporting events and keep candy in our car" religion.

> *(She squirms on the bench.)*

Uuugh, I've got weasels in my stomach.

MOTH: When are your results in?

BERNADETTE: They called yesterday. My appointment's at eight-thirty. I said sit down.

> *(He sits. Beat.)*

MOTH: 'Dette, why do you do it?

BERNADETTE: Jesus Christ, Moth, it's not like smoking. I'm not trying to quit.

> *(Beat.)*

What? What are you thinking?

MOTH: I'm not thinking anything.

BERNADETTE: You have this *look*—

MOTH: There's no look, it's three o'clock in the fucking morning. *I* was sleeping.

BERNADETTE: Don't lie. I know when you're lying.

MOTH: Fine. I'm thinking exactly what I thought the last time, and the time before. I'm thinking you're overreacting.

BERNADETTE: Easy for you to say. Highest risk thing you've ever done was kiss Shelley Fisher when she had a cold sore.

MOTH: Not anymore.

BERNADETTE: By the way, that was really gross—what?

MOTH: You haven't heard. I'm surprised. It's all over school.

BERNADETTE: I skipped.

MOTH: Too bad, I saw Allison in the VP's office this morning, she wanted to make an announcement after "O Canada."

BERNADETTE: You're lying.

MOTH: No, I'm exaggerating. The grapevine was—

BERNADETTE: But I just saw you yesterday.

MOTH: It didn't take very long.

BERNADETTE: Allison?

> *(BERNADETTE starts laughing.)*

MOTH: Oh, I'm glad this is so amusing to you.

BERNADETTE: No, I'm sorry, it's just, Moth, she's a cheerleader.

MOTH: Don't you think I know that?

BERNADETTE: It's just so ... shoo-bop-dee-bop.

MOTH: This is amazing. I have sex, and you think it's cute. *You* wanted this.

BERNADETTE: You did it for me?

MOTH: Bitch. Of course not.

BERNADETTE: So?

MOTH: So what?

BERNADETTE: So give me the details.

MOTH: Why?

BERNADETTE: You know all mine. Your turn.

    (Beat.)

MOTH: Fine. I was at that park party—

BERNADETTE: Oh god.

MOTH: Yeah, and there's your standard guitar-beer-bonfire thing happening—

BERNADETTE: Marshmallows, comfy sweaters, puke puke, go on—

MOTH: And Allison comes up and asks me if I want to take a walk. And I say why—

BERNADETTE: D'uhhh—

MOTH: And she mumbles something about it being Fitness Week. So we're walking around and she's telling me about how her father won't let her wear makeup and we start fooling around and—

BERNADETTE: And?

MOTH: I have to tell *you?*

    (Beat.)

BERNADETTE: So?

MOTH: I don't know. I thought it would be more ... dignified. There were all these elbows and knees ... I lost a sock. You said you weren't going to laugh, Bernadette.

BERNADETTE: I'm not laughing, I'm smirking.

MOTH: That's worse.

BERNADETTE: Allison ... She, she *volunteers* for things.

MOTH: Excuse me, but didn't you date her older brother a few years back? What was his name? *Buck?*

BERNADETTE: Chad.

MOTH: The football player.

BERNADETTE: Rugby. God, I'd almost forgotten. It was so ... clean. I always expected him to offer me a carton of milk afterwards.

> *(Beat.)*

What? I was having a crisis. I wore ribbons in my hair, I stopped masturbating. I was deluded.

MOTH: Did you lose your virginity with him?

BERNADETTE: None of your business.

> *(MOTH is silent.)*

It's not so bad. You get hit by a bus tomorrow, you're a non-virgin with blue hair.

MOTH: Great. Maybe they can put that on my tombstone.

BERNADETTE: Allison's not totally embarassing. She's attractive enough, without audio. Who would you rather have?

MOTH: You. You would have made it more dignified..

BERNADETTE: Don't be stupid. Dignity is not what you're aiming for. What time is it?

MOTH: Three fifty-two.

BERNADETTE: Fuck.

MOTH: Would you breathe? I'll tell you what's going to happen. Exactly what happened the other two times. We go to the Vesta, eat a huge greasy breakfast, walk over to the clinic, you're in and out of there with an HIV negative in fucking thirty seconds and then we ride the adrenalin high for the rest of the day. Go to the park.

BERNADETTE: Fucking right.

MOTH: C'mon, we'll hang upside down on the monkey bars and scream and try not to throw up.

BERNADETTE: Hold my stomach.

> *(MOTH sits behind her and wraps his arms around her waist.)*

MOTH: Okay, go.

BERNADETTE: Animal, vegetable, or mineral?

MOTH: Mineral, sort of.

BERNADETTE: Appliance, building, or natural phenomena?

MOTH: Appliance, sort of.

BERNADETTE: Do you keep me inside or outside your home?

MOTH: Both.

BERNADETTE: I'm an umbrella. You did this one before, moron.

MOTH: Okay, go.

> *(Lights shift. PINCH, wrapped in a sleeping bag, walks across and sits on his front steps.*
>
> *Lights shift. MOTH and BERNADETTE are hanging upside down and screaming.)*

BERNADETTE and MOTH: *(Together.) Aaaahhh!!*

> *(BERNADETTE hops down.)*

BERNADETTE: Thanks.

> *(She kisses MOTH, still upside down, on the mouth. MOTH falls. BERNADETTE starts laughing.)*

MOTH: Don't fucking laugh at me.

BERNADETTE: What?

MOTH: What are you doing?

BERNADETTE: Playing.

MOTH: Yeah, no shit. I'm gonna go.

BERNADETTE: Where?

MOTH: Big building. It's called a school.

> *(MOTH exits. BERNADETTE is alone. She walks towards PINCH, still sitting on his front step.)*

PINCH: AWOL. Where'd you go?

BERNADETTE: Out.

PINCH: Okay.

BERNADETTE: So ... do you have any brothers or sisters?

PINCH: Seven. We're, um—

BERNADETTE: Catholic. I know.

Scene Seven

> *(Afternoon. The bingo hall. MOTH is at the snack counter. BERNADETTE sits on the counter.)*

BERNADETTE: I have never seen so much velour in all my life. Can I yell, "bingo?"

MOTH: You're not playing.

BERNADETTE: Just to screw things up.

MOTH: Shit, here comes my uncle. Your name is Jennifer.

BERNADETTE: Why?

MOTH: Never mind, it just is. And be quiet. People don't come here to talk.

BERNADETTE: I don't want to be Jennifer.

MOTH: So be whoever you want, just get off, I have to wipe the counter down every fifteen minutes.

BERNADETTE: Moth, what's going on?

MOTH: My parents have decided they don't approve of you.

BERNADETTE: What?

MOTH: My stepmother called you evil.

BERNADETTE: Your stepmother tried to make me eat spicy Jello with vegetables in it.

MOTH: She mentioned that when she told me I'm not allowed to see you anymore.

BERNADETTE: Excuse me? What did she say?

MOTH: "Michael, I don't want you to see that Bernadette anymore."

BERNADETTE: Great, I'm a "that." Where is this coming from?

MOTH: The hair, mostly.

BERNADETTE: Why? You blend right in, here.

MOTH: It's not important. I just thought you should know that it's not just the things I do *with* you that are illegal, it's also being near you.

BERNADETTE: Your family is demented.

MOTH: I know, I'm a member. So, are you going to tell me why you haven't phoned me in five days?

BERNADETTE: I've been busy.

MOTH: With what?

BERNADETTE: Stuff.

MOTH: Drug stuff?

BERNADETTE: No.

MOTH: Music stuff?

BERNADETTE: Not exactly. So your folks won't let you see me because I was an accomplice to you dyeing your hair? I'm sorry, Moth, no one is that irrational. There's got to be something else.

MOTH: Hey, do you want some free popcorn? It's my only perk.

BERNADETTE: I'm sensing a lack of communication here.

MOTH: No kidding.

(*Beat.*)

They thought I was gay.

BERNADETTE: What?

MOTH: My parents, they thought I was gay.

BERNADETTE: They told you this?

MOTH: God no. It might give me ideas.

BERNADETTE: I don't follow.

MOTH: Allison stayed for dinner last night.

BERNADETTE: Ohh shit. I leave you alone for five days and look what happens. Look, it's one thing to sleep with someone, Moth, but eating with them—

MOTH: Shut up.

BERNADETTE: But I still—

MOTH: *You* were my parents' proof that I wasn't gay.

BERNADETTE: Finally. A purpose to my life.

MOTH: They never liked you, well, you know, since the Tyler thing. But you were the proof.

BERNADETTE: And now there's Allison.

MOTH: Yes. Allison likes my stepmom's food. Bigger, louder, girlier proof.

BERNADETTE: And I am no longer necessary?

MOTH: Basically.

BERNADETTE: Jesus H. Christ. Dump her.

MOTH: I don't want to. She's nice to me.

BERNADETTE: My *dog* is nice to you.

MOTH: Well, I'm not having sex with your dog.

BERNADETTE: So you're going out with someone because she's as nice as my dog and she'll sleep with you.

MOTH: I didn't say that.

BERNADETTE: Yes, you did.

MOTH: No, I didn't.

(*PINCH enters and holds his hands over BERNADETTE's eyes.*)

BERNADETTE: (*Guessing.*) Some guy that I slept with.

PINCH: Right. Moth, right?

MOTH: Yo.

PINCH: Cool, popcorn, can I have some? I love your hair.

MOTH: Thanks, it was an accident. Bernadette, what's he doing here?

PINCH: I'm her boyfriend.

(*MOTH drops popcorn all over the floor.*)

MOTH: Shit.

PINCH: It's okay, I'll still eat it.

(*PINCH leans down and picks up the popcorn. MOTH leans in to BERNADETTE.*)

MOTH: You said "boyfriend" wasn't a word in your vocabulary.

BERNADETTE: I changed my mind.

MOTH: I don't believe you.

(*MOTH fills a container with popcorn from the floor and hands it to PINCH.*)

Here you go, um—

PINCH: Pinch, thanks.

(*MOTH kneels back down.*)

MOTH: His name is Pinch?

BERNADETTE: It's a long, stupid story.

MOTH: It's a *verb*.

(*PINCH grabs a sheet, walks downstage, and plays bingo intently.*)

MOTH: He—he doesn't have a phone, does he?

BERNADETTE: No.

MOTH: No, no, he'd be one of those cool no-phone guys. No number, they're just *around*.

BERNADETTE: Moth, is there a problem?

MOTH: Problem? Why should I have a fucking problem? I'm a lonely snack-boy at my uncle's bingo hall. I just lost my virginity in a ravine and I have blue hair.

BERNADETTE: So?

MOTH: *My hair is blue*, Bernadette. And this guy walks in and sucks your face and he's suddenly your boyfriend and he eats food off the floor and he plays *bingo*—

BERNADETTE: What's wrong with that?

MOTH: No one under sixty plays bingo, Bernadette. Unless you're brain-damaged or something.

BERNADETTE: He's not brain-damaged.

MOTH: Oh, fine, that's how it works. If you're good-looking, you're not dumb, you're *instinctual.*

BERNADETTE: Where'd you learn a word like that?

MOTH: I am not some kid you babysit! *I am not stupid!*

BERNADETTE: Why are you flipping out?

MOTH: Who made the rules, Bernadette?

BERNADETTE: What fucking rules?

MOTH: Your rules. Your "don't eat with people just fuck them" rules. Your "leave before breakfast" rules. Your fucking rules. *You* made them. But of course they don't apply to you. You can do what ever you want.

BERNADETTE: Yes, I can. Since when do you run my life?

MOTH: Since when do you run mine?

BERNADETTE: Since never.

MOTH: Since you met me. I'm supposed to spill my guts but you can just sit there, *with your shirt off,* implying ... something.

BERNADETTE: I implied nothing.

MOTH: No? What's with this kissing shit all of a sudden?

BERNADETTE: Kissing. Grow up.

MOTH: You're lying.

BERNADETTE: Well, excuse me for not sleeping with a fifteen-year-old just because he wants me to. This is completely irrational. Just, get out of your room, Moth. Go outside. Interact. Get a life.

MOTH: What? Like yours? I don't want your fucking life. You're in grade fourteen and your big claim to fame is that you could suck the chrome off a trailer hitch.

BERNADETTE: I've told you, I don't—

MOTH: You know what they say at school, 'Dette? They're not shocked. They think you're sad.

BERNADETTE: I don't care.

MOTH: Yeah, you don't fucking care. What wakes you up in the middle of the night, 'Dette? You forget to turn the oven off?

(Beat. PINCH begins singing very softly.)

PINCH: Farmer Brown he had a dog and Bingo was his name-o ...

MOTH: You've got a real winner there, 'Dette.

BERNADETTE: Are you just realizing now that I have sex?

MOTH: You didn't even know their last names. Why should I care? What's his middle name?

BERNADETTE: I don't know.

MOTH: Bullshit. I know when you're lying.

BERNADETTE: No you don't.

MOTH: Look, I don't care that you don't sleep with me—okay I do care, but I just think you should tell me what's going on in your life.

BERNADETTE: What, we're discussing our relationship now?

MOTH: No, you can do that with him.

BERNADETTE: Moth—

MOTH: No, you've known him all of five days but I'm sure because *you're fucking him* you owe him some sort of explanation for the fucking demented way you run your life.

BERNADETTE: Shut up.

MOTH: Okay. I can't talk to you anyway or I'll shove popcorn down your stupid fucking throat. Bitch.

BERNADETTE: *(Simultaneously with PINCH's next line.)* Moth. C'mon. Don't do this. I'm—Moth. Please?

PINCH: *(Simultaneously.)* B–I–N–G–O, B–I–N–G–O, B–I–N–G–O, and Bingo was his name-o.

> *(BERNADETTE exits. MOTH and PINCH look at each other. Lights.)*

Scene Eight

> *(Night. MOTH is in his bedroom. He sits on his easy chair, a folded umbrella in his lap. He opens the umbrella and holds it over his head.*
>
> *BERNADETTE is sleeping naked. PINCH is drawing on her body with magic markers. BERNADETTE sits up suddenly, gasping. Beat.)*

BERNADETTE: What are you doing?

PINCH: Making art?

> *(BERNADETTE looks down—PINCH has drawn doodles all over her back and chest.)*

BERNADETTE: Why did you do this?

PINCH: I was bored?

BERNADETTE: You've drawn all over my body.

PINCH: Yes.

BERNADETTE: Don't you think you should ask first?

PINCH: Why?

BERNADETTE: Well, maybe I don't feel like it.

PINCH: You didn't have to feel anything. You were asleep.

BERNADETTE: It's *my* body.

PINCH: I know. But it was there, and you weren't using it, really, so I thought—Look, I did some on the wall, too.

BERNADETTE: So my body is like the wall.

PINCH: Yes. Or no. Your thighs are not fat.

> (*BERNADETTE tries to wipe her face with the sheet.*)

BERNADETTE: Did I say they were?

PINCH: The package says they're washable.

BERNADETTE: My thighs?

PINCH: No, the markers.

BERNADETTE: I'm going outside.

> (*BERNADETTE pulls on a T-shirt and sits outside on the steps. She pulls a safety pin off her necklace and starts pricking her knee. PINCH walks up behind her. She looks back, sees him, and tries to hide what she's doing.*)

PINCH: Don't be scared.

BERNADETTE: I'm not.

PINCH: I used to do that, too.

> (*BERNADETTE looks at her knee, rubbing off the blood.*)

You have to be careful though, if you hit a big vein, blood goes everywhere and people ask questions.

BERNADETTE: You're fucking nuts.

> (*PINCH sits down next to her.*)

PINCH: And when you're done, you're clean.

> (*BERNADETTE tries to wipe the sweat off her face with her T-shirt.*)

So?

BERNADETTE: What?

PINCH: Why'd you wake up?

> (*Beat.*)

BERNADETTE: Nothing. Bad dream.

PINCH: Of what?

BERNADETTE: Why don't you—why don't you go back to sleep.

PINCH: I don't want to.

(PINCH slides his hand around BERNADETTE's waist. BERNADETTE deflates and tries to pull his arm around her stomach.)

You're soaked.

(BERNADETTE stands up. Beat.)

BERNADETTE: You're not getting in, Pinch, so just forget it.

PINCH: Okay, okay, I get it. I'm going to sleep.

(BERNADETTE sits back down.)

BERNADETTE: Thank you. I'm uh … I'm—

PINCH: No problem.

(PINCH bends down to kiss her bleeding knee. BERNADETTE pulls away.)

BERNADETTE: Don't.

(PINCH gets up to leave.)

PINCH: Okay. I love you.

BERNADETTE: Gesundheit.

(Lights shift to MOTH in his bedroom, building something with slides and paper towel rolls.)

Scene Nine

(Afternoon. BERNADETTE is in Moth's bedroom.)

MOTH: How'd you get in?

BERNADETTE: Tyler. *He* still likes me.

(MOTH sits at his desk facing a large fishbowl full of blue marbles. BERNADETTE stands behind him. MOTH begins slowly stuffing marbles in his mouth.)

Moth? I brought dope …

(MOTH turns and glares at her and goes back to his marbles.)

Okay, you're still not talking to me. God, were you a mule in a former life? Fine. Fuck. Um … Okay. How I lost my virginity. Aaaarghh. In Scarborough. I was fifteen. Fifteen sucks rocks, by the way, the only good thing about it is that it *ends*. I was blasted on Rockaberry cooler, I puked tutti-frutti for two days afterwards. His name was Dexter. He had a "Keep on Truckin'" tattoo. We busted a hole in this nice suburban family's waterbed. I caught—a cold.

(MOTH turns and looks at her.)

Okay, it was crabs. So there's the whole story. It's yours. Do what you want with it.

(BERNADETTE stands and kisses MOTH on the cheek. Blue marbles spill out of his mouth.)

MOTH: You're forgiven.

BERNADETTE: And?

MOTH: I'm sorry I said you could suck the chrome off a trailer hitch.

BERNADETTE: That's okay.

MOTH: I meant to say you could suck a golf ball through a garden hose.

BERNADETTE: Moth!

MOTH: You could ... suck-start a Harley.

BERNADETTE: You little shit. Here, roll.

(She tosses the dope tin at him.)

MOTH: Crabs?

BERNADETTE: Crabs are rampant in Scarborough. And if you ever tell anyone, I'll never speak to you again.

(Beat.)

So how are you?

MOTH: Bored. I'm training my eyes to move independently.

BERNADETTE: Of each other?

MOTH: Yeah.

BERNADETTE: How?

MOTH: Paper towel rolls with identical pictures taped on the end—you move them like this until you can focus.

BERNADETTE: Well. That's a career skill.

MOTH: Look what I found.

(He reaches into a box of photographs.)

You with crimped hair.

BERNADETTE: Give that to me!

MOTH: No.

(They wrestle for the photograph. BERNADETTE wins by biting MOTH's leg, grabbing the picture, ripping it into tiny pieces and swallowing them. She picks up the box of photos, and sits on the bed.)

BERNADETTE: You have some problem with photo albums?

MOTH: I hate them. They're like big glossy obituaries.

(BERNADETTE picks up a photo.)

BERNADETTE: What kind of sicko dresses his cat in a doll's clothes?

MOTH: Fluffy got off on it. He had major identity issues.

(Beat.)

BERNADETTE: You look better without braces.

MOTH: Yes, I do.

(MOTH lights up a joint.)

BERNADETTE: How's Allison?

MOTH: She dumped me. She says I used her for sex.

BERNADETTE: Oh.

MOTH: One word about fish and the sea, and I'll break your face.

BERNADETTE: That's ridiculous. It happened like … in spite of you. If anything it's the other way around.

MOTH: How's Pinch?

BERNADETTE: He keeps telling me he loves me.

MOTH: Poor you.

BERNADETTE: It's annoying, it just flies out of his mouth, like it's any old word, like, cutlery, or gearshift.

MOTH: And you?

BERNADETTE: I don't know. You know how I never learned how to dive in swimming?

MOTH: Yeah. Loser.

BERNADETTE: It's kind of the same thing. I'm just not sure I'm into something where my feet go in last.

MOTH: Oh.

(Beat.)

BERNADETTE: It happened once, I think.

(Beat.)

MOTH: With who?

BERNADETTE: The guy who ran the blood donor clinic at school. I saw him walking along the rows of beds, adjusting red tubes and smiling— and he seemed like a lion. I nearly fainted and he fed me Dad's oatmeal cookies and apple juice in a Dixie cup. So I went back, week after week, under assumed names, to donate little plastic bags of blood—so I could see him. And I was dizzy and nauseated and lightheaded, like they say you should be. But I was never sure if it was love … or just anemia.

(Beat.)

Moth?

MOTH: Yeah, yeah, I'm here.

> *(Lights.)*

Scene Ten

> *(Afternoon. BERNADETTE is waiting for PINCH. She stands at a microphone.)*

BERNADETTE: Check. Check mic check. My penis is huge. Check mic check.

> *(PINCH enters.)*

PINCH: Heyy.

BERNADETTE: *(Still into the mic.)* Heyy.

PINCH: I have the best news.

BERNADETTE: Shut up.

PINCH: What?

BERNADETTE: I have been waiting here for three and a half hours.

PINCH: Yeah, sorry about that, Rick and I did mescaline and went to Honest Ed's and it was really hard to leave.

BERNADETTE: *No.* I don't wait, I don't giggle, I do not feign interest in vehicles, sporting events, or computers. This. Is. Not. Who. I. Am.

PINCH: So why didn't you leave?

> *(BERNADETTE steps away from the microphone.)*

BERNADETTE: Good fucking question.

PINCH: 'Cause I gotta motor now, right, I gotta see this guy about a, a thing.

BERNADETTE: I don't believe this. I waited. Pinch, why don't you have a phone?

PINCH: There's these forms you have to fill out, all these little boxes, it's fucking sinister.

> *(PINCH starts packing up the microphone.)*

BERNADETTE: But I wait because you have no phone. There are things I could be doing.

PINCH Like what?

BERNADETTE: Donating organs, I don't know.

PINCH: But guess what?

BERNADETTE: I could mow a lawn. What?

PINCH: We. Are going. On tour.

BERNADETTE: Where?

PINCH: North-western Ontario. MacTier, Parry Sound, Sudbury, Blind River—

BERNADETTE: Oh god.

PINCH: Wawa, Marathon, Schreiber, Thunder Bay. Do you know how many bands have done this?

BERNADETTE: I'd hate to think.

PINCH: What's your problem?

BERNADETTE: You'll, you'll have to take requests, Pinch. You'll have to learn "Yesterday" and "You Picked a Fine Time to Leave Me Lucille."

PINCH: Oh.

BERNADETTE: What?

PINCH: Just, um, do you want to come?

BERNADETTE: I can't go to Marathon. I don't go north of Eglinton.

PINCH: Shit, you can be really boring sometimes.

BERNADETTE: I am not—

PINCH: What's that on your face?

BERNADETTE: What?

PINCH: It's like a vein or something and it's squirming around. Wow, that's really gross. Cool. Bye.

> *(He exits.)*

Scene Eleven

> *(Night. PINCH is in the confessional.)*

PINCH: Bless me father for I have sinned. It's been ten days since my last confession. These are my sins.

> *(Beat.)*

Okay. I've taken drugs, lots, had premarital sex, lots, taken the Lord's name in vain—you know, I keep coming here, and I'm doing Hail Marys for five hours and and it's like—I just don't think I'm naturally a very good person. Like I smoked dope and laughed all through my grandmother's funeral, I pissed in my brother's mouth once, I was an asshole to my girlfriend earlier today, and I'm trying, but at the time, it's like those scrambled cable pornos, right, it's like you think it's maybe a leg, or maybe it's a—well, it's just really warped and you can't tell. Man. What I'm saying is, I miss my high school vice-principal.

'Cause he was this greasy thick-necked bastard in a bad suit and I hated his guts but he had the rules, man, he had them in a plastic binder and every time he said, "I've got my eye on you, young man," I *knew*. It was really *clear*. And now I just keep hoping for floods or earthquakes, you know, like I go and buy my milk and smokes at the 7–Eleven and I fantasize about being caught in a hold-up. 'Cause then it would be *clear*. I could do CPR, or collect cans of beans, or maybe just *remain calm*. Or something. Never mind. Just absolve me and I'll leave you alone.

Scene Twelve

(Night. BERNADETTE storms into Moth's room. MOTH is counting pills and putting all his photos in an album. MOTH does not look up.)

BERNADETTE: Am I boring?

MOTH: Two, four, six.

BERNADETTE: 'Cause I don't think I'm boring. And I hang out with me all the time.

MOTH: Eight, ten.

BERNADETTE: Why do I care? He has no phone, that's fucking abnormal to begin with. Moth, what are you doing?

MOTH: Two, four, six.

BERNADETTE: Oh please, Moth, this is ridiculous.

MOTH: Eight, ten. Why?

BERNADETTE: Because you're doing it all wrong.

MOTH: Eight, ten. Two, four, six.

BERNADETTE: There's no point in dying young, Moth. You'll just get a tacky funeral, a full-page obituary in the *Sun*, and after a few years everyone forgets you ever existed. Like Mike Christie.

MOTH: Eight, ten. Who?

BERNADETTE: See? The guy who O.D.'d last year at the grad party.

MOTH: Two, four, six.

BERNADETTE: Fine. Do it. I dare you. Moth, most people who are going to commit suicide don't wait for company to do it. And pills are really ineffective.

MOTH: Eight, ten.

(As she turns around, MOTH knocks back a handful of pills.)

BERNADETTE: Moth, you fuck!

(BERNADETTE rushes over and expertly does the Heimlich maneuver. MOTH spits out the pills.)

Okay. Can you breathe?

MOTH: You, you think you're so fucking smart—

BERNADETTE: Just hold still—

MOTH: You've got it all figured out, you fucking—

BERNADETTE: Just breathe, shit—

(He grabs a pencil off his desk and tries to stab his arm.)

MOTH: You think you always know *exactly what I'm going to do*—

BERNADETTE: Moth!

(They struggle. MOTH's arm is bleeding. She holds his arms behind him. MOTH deflates.)

Shut up and breathe.

(MOTH sits still. BERNADETTE strokes his hair back from his forehead. Beat. BERNADETTE kneels beside and takes his bleeding arm and tries to suck out a piece of lead.)

MOTH: *(Quietly.)* You know, your mouth is one of the dirtiest parts of your body.

(BERNADETTE extracts a piece of lead with her teeth.)

Ow!

(Beat.)

I'm sorry.

BERNADETTE: It's okay.

(She begins cleaning the pills off the desk.)

Fuck me. These are orange-flavoured Children's Tylenol.

MOTH: So?

BERNADETTE: You can't O.D. on something chewable, Moth.

MOTH: Why not?

BERNADETTE: Well, besides being totally hilarious, it's just not possible.

MOTH: You are such a cow. I hope you catch fire.

BERNADETTE: I didn't think you were serious.

MOTH: No shit.

BERNADETTE: So what is it?

(Beat.)

MOTH: I'm really, really … bored.

BERNADETTE: No, you're not.

MOTH: Yes, I am.

> *(BERNADETTE starts taking the photos out of his album and throw-*
> *ing them on his bed.)*

BERNADETTE: You're not bored. You're just precocious. It's that gifted
program, it fucked you up.

MOTH: No. What does a precocious forty-five-year-old do? Take up
shuffleboard? Move into a nursing home? No, I flashed forward on my
life, I just saw this tepid, grey, capital-L Liberal—in bed by eleven—
Sears Portrait Studio children existence looming ahead of me. *And* I'm
going bald.

> *(BERNADETTE inspects his head.)*

BERNADETTE: Wow, you are precocious.

> *(Beat.)*

I'm not going to tell you eveything's going to be okay.

> *(MOTH leans forward and kisses her.)*

Moth—

MOTH: Please?

> *(BERNADETTE walks him over so he's standing by the bed covered*
> *in snapshots. She takes off his shirt. Lights out.*
>
> *Night. BERNADETTE sits up, gasping. She sees MOTH's sleeping*
> *body next to hers.)*

BERNADETTE: Oh shit. Fuck. Shit. Shit. Shit. Shit.

> *(Beat.)*

I'm sorry …

> *(Lights out.*
>
> *Night. PINCH gasps and clasps his hands over his eyes.*
>
> *Morning. BERNADETTE is scrambling across the floor for her*
> *clothes. MOTH sits up.)*

MOTH: Hi.

BERNADETTE: Hi.

MOTH: Do you have to go meet Pinch?

BERNADETTE: No, no. He's pretty busy these days, you know, he's
taking the band on tour. To Wawa.

MOTH: That's not a real place.

BERNADETTE: Yes, it is.

MOTH: I guess that's what you get for dating a musician.

BERNADETTE: Yeah, it's like dating a drug dealer. Everything seems fine and then you get seven Quaaludes for Christmas.

MOTH: That's funny.

BERNADETTE: Thanks.

> *(Beat.)*

No, I just figured, you know, I should get out of your hair before your parents—

MOTH: No, actually, they've gone golfing.

BERNADETTE: Oh, oh great.

MOTH: Yeah.

> *(Beat.)*

BERNADETTE: Would you like your shirt?

> *(She hands it to him. He puts it on.)*

I'm gonna—

MOTH: 'Dette—

BERNADETTE: Go.

Scene Thirteen

> *(Morning. PINCH crouches, shaking, his hands over his eyes. Enter BERNADETTE.)*

BERNADETTE: Pinch? Where are you?

PINCH: *Ssshhh!!*

BERNADETTE: *(Whispering.)* What are you doing?

PINCH: I'm hiding.

BERNADETTE: You're what?

PINCH: Hide! They can see you.

BERNADETTE: Ohh, fuck, Pinch, what did you take last night?

PINCH: Stop saying my name!

BERNADETTE: What did you—

PINCH: I didn't take anything! I don't do drugs. I'm clean, I'm a very clean boy.

BERNADETTE: Whatever.

PINCH: Come hide under here with me.

BERNADETTE: No, no, I'm okay. I've uh … got a gun.

PINCH: Wow, you're so cool.

BERNADETTE: How long have you been here?

PINCH: You know, Father Patrick told me, but I didn't listen.

BERNADETTE: He told you what?

PINCH: See, you're not listening either! You don't *listen*, Bernadette—

BERNADETTE: You haven't—

PINCH: He *said* ... Are you listening?

BERNADETTE: Yes.

PINCH: He said that the only thing, the *only thing* that seperates us from the animals is that *we know someone is watching.*

BERNADETTE: Jesus Christ. Pinch, I'm gonna go find Rick or something.

PINCH: Ohhh. I want to go home.

BERNADETTE: You are home.

PINCH: Nooo. Home.

BERNADETTE: Where's home.

PINCH: New Liskeard. I gotta go home. I gotta go back to high school, finish grade nine—

BERNADETTE: Pinch?

PINCH: *Shhh!!*

BERNADETTE: Sorry.

PINCH: I gotta go to the high school and wish my sister happy birthday. Three times.

BERNADETTE: Pinch, look at me.

PINCH: I'm hiding!

BERNADETTE: From who?

PINCH: You know. I didn't know he was retarded.

BERNADETTE: Who?

PINCH: My cousin, big black-haired kid at Christmas. The Mitterons' boy, he was home for the holidays—I thought he was drunk.

BERNADETTE: And he wasn't.

PINCH: Nooo ... And me and my brothers were following him around, imitating him, and I—pushed him, on his face in the dirty snow with all the beer cans and his mom was watching the whole thing from the back porch and crying—

BERNADETTE: Did you get in trouble?

PINCH: No! They just kept saying, "It's okay, Jacques, you didn't know, how could you know, it's not your fault, it's not," but if it's not my fucking fault then why is she crying?

BERNADETTE: Did you say you were sorry?

PINCH: I tried. But you know, it was time for presents.

BERNADETTE: You were just a kid.

PINCH: But I knew to be sorry. Ohhh no. I'm sorry. I'm sorry.

BERNADETTE: Pinch—

PINCH: Say it! I'm sorry.

BERNADETTE: I'm sorry.

> *(Beat. BERNADETTE takes his hands away from his eyes.)*

Okay?

PINCH: Okay. But I need to go home.

BERNADETTE: Now?

PINCH: I need to apologize.

BERNADETTE: Pinch, it was years ago.

PINCH: I need to.

> *(Beat.)*

Can I borrow twenty dollars?

> *(BERNADETTE takes money out of her pocket and hands it to him. PINCH stands up.)*

Whoa ... I have to go to the bus station now.

BERNADETTE: Wait. What about all your stuff?

PINCH: Oh, it's not mine, really, I dumpster-dived it.

BERNADETTE: Oh.

PINCH: Thanks for the money.

BERNADETTE: Whatever.

PINCH: I have to leave. I love you.

BERNADETTE: Shut up.

PINCH: Okay. Bye.

> *(He exits, leaving BERNADETTE alone in the room.)*

Scene Fourteen

> *(Morning. PINCH walks out of his apartment and MOTH is sitting on the steps, playing with his "independent eye" tubes.)*

PINCH: Moth.

MOTH: Hi.

PINCH: What are you doing here?

MOTH: Looking for Bernadette.

PINCH: You have to ring the doorbell.

MOTH: I know.

PINCH: She's just inside.

MOTH: I know.

> *(PINCH sits down next to him.)*

PINCH: You slept with her, didn't you?

MOTH: Are you going to hit me?

PINCH: Nah.

MOTH: Where are you going?

PINCH: Home, I think.

MOTH: You're going the wrong way.

PINCH: No, back home. New Liskeard.

> *(He grabs Moth's "independent eyes" tubes and looks through them.)*

MOTH: Don't—

PINCH: Man, you are one warped little kid.

MOTH: I'm not a kid.

PINCH: Sure you are. Nothing wrong with it.

> *(MOTH grabs his tubes back and stuffs them in his backpack.)*

MOTH: You don't know her.

> *(Beat.)*

PINCH: Man, I feel like I *should* hit you.

> *(MOTH leans over and deliberately kisses PINCH on the mouth.)*

What the?

MOTH: I just—I just wanted to make a circle.

> *(PINCH stands, baffled. MOTH flashes him a huge grin.)*

I'm going to go ring the doorbell now.

> *(Lights.)*

Scene Fifteen

> *(MOTH walks into Pinch's room. BERNADETTE is frantically cleaning.)*

MOTH: Hi.

(BERNADETTE *looks up.*)

BERNADETTE: Oh god. Hi, Moth.

MOTH: What are you doing?

BERNADETTE: This place is a huge mess.

MOTH: Oh ... Do you need some help?

> (BERNADETTE *shrugs and continues cleaning.* MOTH *helps her. Beat.*)

'Dette, did someone die?

BERNADETTE: No.

MOTH: Then why are we talking like this?

BERNADETTE: Like what?

MOTH: Like we're being videotaped.

> (*Beat.*)

BERNADETTE: Moth, it was a one-time thing, okay? I'm sorry if I—well I'm just sorry.

MOTH: You're *sorry.*

BERNADETTE: If I could do it again—

MOTH: So you regret it. Oh, that makes me feel so much better.

BERNADETTE: I don't mean it that way.

> (*Beat.*)

MOTH: I ran into Pinch outside.

BERNADETTE: Ignore him, he's fucked on something.

MOTH: Did you give him money?

BERNADETTE: Yeah. Can I borrow twenty dollars?

MOTH: Why's he going home?

BERNADETTE: He has to apologize to someone.

MOTH: Him too?

BERNADETTE: So what's your solution for a mistake?

MOTH: Don't call it a mistake.

BERNADETTE: Mistake.

MOTH: Shut up.

BERNADETTE: Mistake.

MOTH: I don't hear you—

BERNADETTE: Moth, I was your babysitter!

MOTH: Five fucking years ago!

BERNADETTE: But, but still, you had a bedtime, and—and a milk carton collection and now we're—we're—

MOTH: Having sex. And you're sorry.

BERNADETTE: I don't want to mess you up.

MOTH: No, no, I'm fine. I'm just going to build a huge fucking wing and live under it for the rest of my life.

BERNADETTE: Moth—

MOTH: So at what point did you start to regret it?

BERNADETTE: You're not being—

MOTH: No, I'd like to know. Was it when you woke up? Halfway through? As soon as it happened?

BERNADETTE: I didn't mean it that way.

MOTH: I'd just like to know how long you were with me, and how long you were just humouring me.

BERNADETTE: I was not humouring you.

MOTH: Good. Because—

BERNADETTE: Because what?

MOTH: Nothing.

BERNADETTE: No. Tell me.

MOTH: Because you're not as good in bed as I thought you would be.

BERNADETTE: Oh. Man.

MOTH: Sorry.

> *(Beat.)*

BERNADETTE: Moth, I think I should leave you alone.

MOTH: What?

BERNADETTE: Moth, don't you fucking get it? I am a really shitty role model. I've never grown out of anything but clothes.

MOTH: You think you offer me guidance?

BERNADETTE: I think I try.

MOTH: You think I listen?

BERNADETTE: You know you do.

> *(Beat.)*

MOTH: It's not that fucking clear.

BERNADETTE: I need a fresh start.

MOTH: So shave your head.

BERNADETTE: It's your life to fuck up, Moth. And I hate watching you fall on your ass, but I can't help looking. You're my personal car wreck.

(Beat.)

Moth? Say something, please. Moth, I've thought about this a lot.

MOTH: Yeah, all morning.

(Beat.)

Okay.

BERNADETTE: What?

MOTH: I'll go. Just don't talk to me and I won't bug you. I promise.

(He exits, leaving behind the tubes, but stands in the hallway watching her. BERNADETTE thinks she is alone. She picks up the tubes and looks through them.)

BERNADETTE: Oh god.

(MOTH walks back into the room.)

You fuck. These are pictures of me.

MOTH: I have to keep an eye on you. You're asking me to go around half-blind. You can't do that.

BERNADETTE: Moth—

MOTH: You are such a stupid cow. You're sorry? Okay, fine, I forgive you.

BERNADETTE: How can you do that?

MOTH: I don't know.

(Beat.)

Can you focus?

BERNADETTE: No.

(He demonstrates how they work, standing behind her and moving them slowly apart. Lights shift to PINCH in the confessional.)

PINCH: Bless me father for I have sinned. It's been two days since my last confession. These are my sins.

(Beat.)

Okay, I've taken more drugs, had more premarital—shit. Sorry. Look, I took off today because I was scared, and I think it's the worst thing I've done this week. But you, you don't even consider that a sin, although maybe you'd absolve me if I asked. And I have no idea whose fault it was, so I have no idea where to put the blame. And this blame thing seems pretty big to you, I blame me, or the devil, if it's major, and you take the blame away. But I think I want to keep it. 'Cause these days it's like I can see blame, thick and yellow like mustard, being spread around my life. And you're up there, acting like some universal spot remover, sucking it up and away. And I'm thinking, if we each could just keep it, you know, like carry a little yellow stain on our jeans, and fucking leave it there, well, maybe I'd feel okay. Just to have the stain, on my knee, and when people asked I could say, "Oh, that's just a bit of blame." And for it I am truly, truly sorry.

(Lights shift back to BERNADETTE, with MOTH holding the tubes over her eyes.)

MOTH: Can you focus?

BERNADETTE: Yes—

MOTH: See, 'Dette? See how far you can go?

(Blackout. The end.)

About the Playwrights

MARIE CLEMENTS is a performer and writer based in Vancouver. Her other plays include *Age of Iron* (Firehall Arts Centre, 1993), *The Girl Who Swam Forever* (UBC/Savage Media, 1995), and *Urban Tattoo* (Women in View Festival, 1998). Her most recent play, *The Unnatural and Accidental Women,* is based on the murder by forced alcohol consumption of several Native women in Vancouver by a white barber over the span of thirty years. Marie is currently adapting *The Unnatural and Accidental Women* into a novel.

VIVIENNE LAXDAL resides in the Gatineau Hills where she writes plays and other things. She has been resident playwright at the Centaur Theatre in Montreal and an invited member of the Playwrights Units at the Great Canadian Theatre Company (Ottawa) and Toronto's Canadian Stage Company. She is a past winner of a CBC Radio Drama Competition, a Canadian Authors Association Award, and was awarded first place in the Canadian National Playwriting Competition for her play *Karla and Grif.* Her other plays include *These Girls, National Capitale Nationale, Personal Convictions,* and *Goose Spit.*

KATE MILES'S one-act play *Homing Pigeons* premièred at the 1998 Rhubarb! Festival at Buddies in Bad Times Theatre. She has written short plays for the Tarragon Spring Arts Fair and Shaw Festival Academy, including *H is for Hamster, Amoeba, Speak of My Devil,* and *Really Really Bad Words* (co-written with Fabrizio Filippo), as well as contributing monologues for *Growing Crooked* at the Annex Theatre. Kate was a member of the 1992 Tarragon Chalmers Playwright Unit and playwright-in-residence during the 1992-93 season.

KELLEY JO BURKE is an award-winning playwright, poet, and broadcaster. While she's yet to be nominated for any awards for it, she is also the mother of two children. Her play *Charming and Rose: True Love* was a finalist for the Dora and Chalmers Award for the best new play in 1993. Her other plays include *Fat Girls (wear all sizes), Goddessness,* and a number of radio plays for the CBC, including the award-winning *Jane's Thumb.* Her poetry has appeared in *Grain* and *The Fiddlehead,* and she is a regular contributor to *Contemporary Verse 2.* As a broadcaster she works as a film critic, commentator, and producer, and has written three documentaries for CBC Radio's *Ideas.* She is past president of the Saskatchewan Playwrights Centre, and the current Women's Caucus chair of the Playwrights' Union of Canada. She was the 1997 and the 1992 recipient of the City of Regina Writing Award.

TOBY RODIN's one woman show, *Horseradish for Robert,* premièred in London, England and toured across Canada as part of the Fringe Festival circuit. She has studied at Ecole Jacques LeCoq. and has been a member of the Tarragon Playwright's Unit. She has also attended the Banff Playwrights Colony where she first began work on *The Slow Eviction of Ruby Rosenholtz,* her first full-length play. Toby Rodin lives in Toronto.